# THE DOWNFALL OF CARTESIANISM
## 1673–1712

ARCHIVES INTERNATIONALES D'HISTOIRE DES IDEES

INTERNATIONAL ARCHIVES OF THE HISTORY OF IDEAS

11

RICHARD A. WATSON

# THE DOWNFALL OF CARTESIANISM
## 1673-1712

A STUDY OF EPISTEMOLOGICAL ISSUES IN LATE
17TH CENTURY CARTESIANISM

RICHARD A. WATSON

*Assistant Professor*

*Washington University*

# THE DOWNFALL OF CARTESIANISM
## 1673-1712

A STUDY OF EPISTEMOLOGICAL ISSUES IN LATE
17TH CENTURY CARTESIANISM

MARTINUS NIJHOFF – THE HAGUE – 1966

PRINTED IN THE NETHERLANDS

# ACKNOWLEDGEMENTS

An earlier version of this book was written as a dissertation under the direction of Professor Richard H. Popkin, now Chairman of the Department of Philosophy at the University of California, San Diego. I have benefitted immensely from his knowledge of 17th century philosophy and his willingness to discuss the issues considered here. Popkin's major work, *The History of Scepticism from Erasmus to Descartes* (Assen: Van Gorcum, 1960; revised edition, 1964) provides the necessary background for the present study.

Professors Harry M. Bracken of Arizona State University and Edwin B. Allaire of the University of Iowa have read the manuscript in several stages of completion; each has made valuable comments. I wish also to thank my professors at the University of Iowa, my fellow students there (now professors) Henry G. Van Leeuwen of Hanover College and Philip D. Cummins of the University of Iowa, my former colleagues at the University of Michigan, and my wife, all of whom have assisted me in the completion of this study. Further invaluable help has been provided by the secretarial staff of the Department of Philosophy at the University of Michigan and by many librarians of the following libraries: Library of the University of Iowa, Library of the University of Michigan, Niedersächsischen Landesbibliothek, Bibliothèque Nationale, Honnold Library of the Associated Colleges at Claremont, Hoose Library of Philosophy of the University of Southern California.

Permission has kindly been granted by the editors of the *Revue internationale de la philosophie* and the *Journal of the History of Philosophy* for the publication of material which has appeared in different form in their journals.

Research funds were supplied by a University of Michigan Horace H. Rackham Graduate School Summer Faculty Research Fellowship and Research Grant. Funds for typing the manuscript were provided by the Department of Philosophy at the University of Michigan.

# TABLE OF CONTENTS

# CHAPTER I

# INTRODUCTION

Phenomenalism, idealism, spiritualism, and other contemporary philosophical movements originating in the reflective experience of the *cogito* witness to the immense influence of Descartes. However, Cartesianism as a complete metaphysical system in the image of that of the master collapsed early in the 18th century. A small school of brilliant Cartesians, almost all expert in the new mechanistic science, flashed like meteors upon the intellectual world of late 17th century France to win well-deserved recognition for Cartesianism. They were accompanied by a scintillating comet, Malebranche, the deviant Cartesian, now remembered as the orthodox Cartesians are not. However, all these bright lights faded upon the philosophical horizon, almost as soon as they appeared. The metaphysical dualism of Descartes was, as such, neither to be preserved nor reconstructed.

There are many reasons why the Cartesian system did not survive the victory over Scholasticism which Descartes, Malebranche, and the others had won. Newtonian physics very soon replaced Cartesian physics. The practical interest and success of the new science which the Cartesians themselves had nurtured drew men down from the lofty realms of metaphysics. On the popular front, Cartesianism was attacked and ridiculed for the view that animals are unthinking machines. In the schools of Paris and elsewhere, there was the general but severe opposition of pedants, which is perhaps of more historical than philosophical interest. The Church put Descartes' *Méditations* on the Index, and the Cartesian explanation of transubstantiation was taken as an attack upon Church tradition, if not upon Church doctrine.

The most important reason for the rapid fall of the Cartesian metaphysical system is that it is philosophically inadequate in many ways. Criticisms of these inadequacies came from varied sources during the second half of the 17th century and are so thorough that the close of the century is also the close of the Cartesian era. Problems within the system derive primarily from conflicts among Cartesian principles. The major difficulties stem from the dualistic system of mind and matter in which the ontological categories of substance and modification are exhaustive, and which includes epistemological and causal likeness principles. If the representation must be in some way like the object represented, and the cause in some way like the effect, then the Cartesian metaphysical system incorporates an unbridgeable gulf between mind and matter. The Cartesians, orthodox and deviant alike, could explain neither how two substances unlike in essence could causally interact, nor how one could know the other.

The main attack came from a source the Cartesians at first refused to take seriously. L'Abbé Simon Foucher, Chanoine de la Sainte Chapelle de Dijon, was an eccentric and obscure sceptic; he said he was an Academic in the tradition of Socrates and Philo. He wrote several critical works, making in each more or less the same points against Cartesian metaphysics. Foucher's sceptical technique is to admit the Cartesian ontological principles, and then to show that contradictions arise when they are combined with Cartesian epistemological and causal principles. According to these principles, Foucher argues, it should be impossible for mind and matter to interact, and for mind to know matter. In fact, however, we experience the interaction and have the knowledge. Thus, Foucher concludes, the Cartesian metaphysical system is based on false principles. Its major systemic breakdown derives from the inability of Cartesians to perfect an epistemology commensurate with their ontology.

How can two unlike substances causally interact? How can mind know matter? The two major answers offered by the Cartesians are developed from either the denial of the likeness principles or the alteration of the ontological framework. Neither of these answers is intelligible within the Cartesian context. Ultimately, the Cartesians appealed to God to support the Cartesian machine. Certainly God is far from being extraneous in Cartesianism. Many opponents, however, thought it unphilosophical to hark to His inexplicable ways to explain events which are evidently impossible according to Cartesian principles.

*The Downfall of Cartesianism* is thus a study of failure. Its binding thread is the development of the Cartesian way of ideas in the face of these problems. It follows the fortunes of Cartesianism through the critical years from 1673, when Simon Foucher published his first critique, to 1712, when Malebranche published the last additions to his system. The body of this study is historical; its heart is a logical analysis of how and why the Cartesians failed to solve their problems. The analysis deals primarily with Foucher's criticisms of Cartesian metaphysics. My purpose is to show that Cartesian failures to answer Foucher's sceptical objections led to the downfall of the Cartesian metaphysical system. The arguments Foucher originated became thereafter very important in the history of modern philosophy. Bayle included them in his *Dictionnaire*, and those against the distinction between primary and secondary qualities were taken from Bayle for explosive use by Berkeley and Hume. Thus, the further development of the way of ideas is followed through Locke, Berkeley, and Hume in order to show what the post-Cartesians believed was necessary to replace Cartesian metaphysics as a whole.

There has been one other major study which shows reasons for the downfall of Cartesianism. Professor Norman Kemp Smith[1] argues that Cartesianism as a complete metaphysical system failed because causal relations cannot be rationalized. He carries his study through Hume and Kant to show that the Cartesian dream is impossible of realization. Cartesians wanted to have a logic which exactly represents the world, an axiomatic system of ideas from which absolutely certain conclusions can be deduced about the world. Not only must the ideas truly represent the essences of things in the world, the relations of logical necessity in the deductive system must also truly represent necessary causal relations in the world. Kemp Smith's argument is that the downfall of Cartesianism is due to the fact that necessary logical relations in deductive systems are eternal, whereas necessary causal relations (if there are such) in the world are temporal. Cartesian rationalism must inevitably fail because eternal relations in logic can not be representations of temporal relations in the world.

I have little argument with Kemp Smith's conclusions. He illuminates one major defect, sufficient for the failure of Cartesianism. I illuminate another major defect, and show that not only is it a sufficient reason, it is also the actual cause of the downfall of Cartesian metaphysics. This defect is that the Cartesians could give no intelligible explanation of how ideas represent their objects. Their inability is traced to two connected aspects of traditional substance philosophy.

First, the Cartesians are bound to the notion that representation depends upon or is the same as resemblance or likeness between an idea

[1] Smith, Norman Kemp, *Studies in the Cartesian Philosophy* (London: Macmillan, 1902).

(whatever it is) and the object it represents. Part of my argument for this rests on evidence that they are bound also to the notion that causal interaction depends upon likeness between cause and effect. When the later Cartesians abandoned the principles that there must be likeness between an idea and its object, and between a cause and its effect, they could no longer explain how mental ideas could represent material objects, nor how a mind could causally interact with a body.

Second, the Cartesians have a notion of a mind's being directly acquainted with ideas which makes direct acquaintance dependent upon or identical with the relation of a substance to its modifications. The Cartesians never doubted that a mind has knowledge of its own ideas which are *in* the mind as modifications of it, since it seemed to them obvious that a mind is directly acquainted with its own modifications. When they abandoned the notion that ideas are mental modifications, the Cartesians could no longer explain how a mind could be directly acquainted with and thus know ideas.

The downfall of Cartesianism, then, comes because criticism of the Cartesian metaphysical system led to demands for an explanation of representation not based on resemblance of idea to object, an explanation of causal interaction not dependent on likeness between mind and body, and an explanation of direct acquaintance which does not make it identical with the relation of a substance to its modifications. The Cartesians could provide no such explanations.

It can now be pointed out that Kemp Smith comes to the conclusions he does because he also accepts the principle that resemblance is necessary for representation. He insists that eternal, i.e., timeless, logical relations cannot represent temporal causal relations because of the lack of resemblance between them. It is enough here to say on this subject that a deep-seated philosophical concern underlying the present study is embodied in the question: *Is* resemblance necessary for representation?

In broad terms, we move in this study from a consideration of problems arising from an ontology of two substances different in essence, to a consideration of problems arising from an ontology of two categories, substance and modification. The Cartesians were concerned with relationships between two substances, but they saw no difficulties connected with the relationship between a substance and its properties or modifications. Berkeley's treatment (deriving from Malebranche) of the relationships between mind and idea, and between mind and notion, is illuminated by a consideration of the extent to which he took these relationships for granted in the Cartesian way (as substance to modification), and of the extent to which he saw difficulties in the relationship between substance and modification. The Berkeleian solution to Cartesian problems by the introduction of an entity external to substance and modification, like that of Malebranche before him, was not successful; Malebranche belittled, and Berkeley denied the dualism of substances, but neither philosopher could break entirely with the ontological pattern of substance and modification. The final breakdown of Cartesian metaphysics came with Hume, who, in completely abandoning the ontology of substance and modification, parted company with substance philosophy and became the father of contemporary philosophy.

*The Downfall of Cartesianism 1673–1712* may thus seem a title both too broad and too narrow for what is covered herein. However, it is the best title within the limits of 20th century (as opposed to 17th century) scholarly conventions. In using it, I stress that after the publication of the last of Malebranche's *Eclaircissements* in 1712 the ascendancy of the complete dualistic Cartesian metaphysical system was done. That is, by then the sceptical critics had exposed problems the Cartesians could not solve. However, no claim is made that all aspects of Cartesianism disappeared or stopped developing, for it is evident that much of Western philosophy today is in a very broad sense Cartesian. And of course the other factors mentioned earlier contributed to the downfall of the metaphysical system. Nevertheless, I do claim that the more strictly epistemological difficulties studied herein are crucial philosophically.

The narrowness of the title is seen from another viewpoint. The downfall of Cartesianism is intimately linked to the inadequacies of substance philosophy. Malebranche recognized at least vaguely the ontological paucity of a system which makes the categories of *substance* and *modification* all-inclusive. The major failures of the Cartesians are traced to their inability to break out of this ontological pattern. Philosophers later in the Cartesian tradition did break with this pattern and in carrying this study through Hume, I have shown that the downfall of Cartesianism is a major movement toward the collapse of a strain of substance philosophy which Descartes inherited from his Scholastic predecessors.

Although Descartes' substance philosophy derives from Scholastic patterns, the Cartesian system is in many respects developed in opposition to Scholastic explanations in physics and particularly to those

of perception. Therefore, it will be useful to give here a short characterization of a Scholastic theory of perception. The Aristotelian account
presented is essentially that of St. Thomas Aquinas,[1] though it is
clear from the Cartesian attacks that the Peripatetics were variously
interpreted. Some of the arguments for and against the Cartesian
theory of perception even take as a foil a theory more Epicurean than
Aristotelian.

All material substances, goes the Thomistic account, are composed
of a union of form which is a principle of organization and of matter
which has a capacity to be organized. Each particular material thing
or substance necessarily has only one essential form which gives the
thing the being it has. Substantial change can occur when one essential
form replaces another, the matter remaining the same. Besides its
essential form, a material thing can have an unspecified number of
accidental forms or qualities. Traditionally, these are reducible to
the four sets of opposites: heat and cold, wetness and dryness, dense-
ness and rarity, heaviness and lightness. The first of each pair is an
active quality which can act on its passive opposite; the quantitative
proportions of these qualities in the thing determine its nature. By
Descartes' time the ranks of accidental forms were swollen with any
number of occult powers, real accidents, sensible qualities, thisnesses,
and so on. Each of these qualities, when actually qualifying a thing,
excludes all other qualities of its same general kind; that is, whiteness
in a material thing causes it to be white, and greenness (nor any other
color) cannot be in the thing in the same way at the same time as
whiteness, and so on. It should be noted that the thing remains sub-
stantially the same whatever accidental forms qualify it, so long as the
essential form which gives it being as a substance remains the same.
Of the essential forms which give being to material substances, only
one can exist separately from union with matter. This unique substantial form is the human soul. Matter itself is featureless, without
quantity, extension, or dimension, until united with form; however,
since its priority is only logical, matter cannot exist outside the union.

The central point in the Thomistic account of perception is that the
sense organs and the intellect can in some way receive the essential
form of a material thing or substance without its matter. In the process
of knowing, the impossibility of a substance having more than one
form is in some way transcended as the knower takes on besides his own

[1] For a more expanded account see, e.g., Chapters IX and X of S. J. Curtis' *A Short History of Western Philosophy in the Middle Ages* (London: MacDonald & Co., Ltd., 1950).

essential form the form of the known, and the known shares its form with the knower. The mechanics of this process are complicated. In a knowing situation, there must be the knower, the material thing known, and a medium. The material thing expresses itself through the medium to cause a material impression upon the sense organ. This impression causes Imagination to form sense imagery consisting of a material image or phantasm. The Active Intellect illumines the sense imagery, abstracting from it to form in the Possible Intellect the intelligible species which is the essential form of the thing known; this essential form exists in the Possible Intellect with intentional being, while at the same time it exists in and gives natural being to the thing known. Thus, the thing itself is known through the intelligible species, which amounts to knowing directly the thing's essential form. If, in reflection, the intelligible species itself is made the object of thought, it is referred to by a mental word, a concept.

Three aspects of this explanation should be noted. The first intention in knowing is the essential form of the thing known; the intelligible species is not a representative being as such, but the known essence. One is conscious of representative concepts only in representing the intelligible species themselves, objects of second intention. Second, the Scholastic contention that the action of the material thing causes a material image to be conducted through the medium to the sense organs is so far like the Cartesian mechanical account of perception. In either case, it is clear that no Epicurean material species travels from the thing known to the knower. The Scholastics then require that the phantasm formed by Imagination contain as abstractable the essential form or intelligible species of the thing to be known. For the Scholastics, what is known is not something which simply belongs to the knower; the intelligible species *is* the essential form of the thing known shared by the knower. But in the Cartesian account, the idea which arises is only a modification of the mind, which is not the same as, nor even essentially like, the known thing's form as the Cartesians understand it. Third, upon the Scholastic account of perception the significance of the maxim. *Nihil est in intellectu quod non prius fuerit in sensu,* is apparent. If material things did not act through a medium upon the sense organs, nothing would be known. But the maxim does not mean that anything sensible or material is found in the Intellect; what is known are immaterial natures.

For the Scholastics, sensible qualities actually modify material things. These properties may be only non-essential accidents, but they do exist in material things *as* they are sensed. The Cartesians object strenuously to this categorization. They feel that it leads to inconsistencies and absurdities. In its place they offer a distinction which in one form is later popularized by Locke as the distinction between primary and secondary qualities. The Cartesian distinction between modifications of the body and modifications of the mind, and the subsidiary distinction between sensations and ideas, are the major tools for dislodging Scholastic physics. They are also to be used in providing an infallible way of knowing material things. Foucher examines these Cartesian distinctions to make major criticisms of the Cartesian way of knowing by ideas. And since the distinctions are an essential part of the foundations of Cartesian metaphysics, the inadequacies exposed by Foucher reflect the basic inadequacies of Cartesianism. Since the distinction between primary and secondary qualities plays a central role in the following chapters, we shall examine briefly its development before Descartes.

The distinction between primary and secondary qualities is generally taken to be a differentiation of sensible qualities from mathematical qualities. The sensible or secondary qualities are colors, odors, tastes, sounds, and tactual feelings including pleasure, pain, heat, and cold, that is, all the objects of our senses. Mathematical qualities include size, shape, and motion or rest, that is, all properties of material things which are amenable to quantitative or mathematical representation. The distinction could still be made even if it were claimed – as the Scholastics do – that material things have as their properties both primary and secondary qualities, and further, that the mathematical qualities are also sensible.

In the Cartesian tradition the distinction is much more profound than it can be made in Scholastic terms. Descartes finds the secondary quality and its perception to be one; sensation and sensible quality are the same; the object of a sensation, inasmuch as it has one, is the sensation itself. And since sensations are modifications of the immaterial mind, material things have none of the secondary qualities as such. They do have, however, the primary qualities of which we have ideas but not sensations. To speak of secondary qualities in material things for Descartes, as for Locke, is either to speak falsely or to refer to those collections of primary qualities which give rise to sensations in our minds when material things interact with our sense organs.

One of the first modern expressions of the distinction is found in Galileo's *Il Saggiatore*. He reasons as follows:

I want to propose some examination of that which we call heat, whose generally accepted notion comes very far from the truth if my serious doubts be correct, inasmuch as it is supposed to be a true accident, affection, and quality really residing in the thing which we perceive to be heated. Nevertheless I say, that indeed I feel myself impelled by the necessity, as soon as I conceive a piece of matter or corporeal substance, of conceiving that in its own nature it is bounded and figured in such and such a figure, that in relation to others it is large or small, that it is in this or that place, in this or that time, that it is in motion or remains at rest, that it touches or does not touch another body, that it is single, few, or many; in short by no imagination can a body be separated from such conditions; but that it must be white or red, bitter or sweet, sounding or mute, of a pleasant or unpleasant odour, I do not perceive my mind forced to acknowledge it necessarily accompanied by such conditions; so if the senses were not the escorts, perhaps the reason or the imagination by itself would never have arrived at them. Hence I think that these tastes, odours, colours, etc., on the side of the object in which they seem to exist, are nothing else than mere names, but hold their residence solely in the sensitive body; so that if the animal were removed, every such quality would be abolished and annihilated.[1]

Galileo goes on to say that all that is needed "to excite in us these tastes, these odours, and these sounds" is "size, figure, number, and slow or rapid motion." [2] Heat in the material thing is nothing more than the rapid motion of minute bodies. Without a living animal having sense organs in active contact with material things, there would be no sensations or secondary qualities. Galileo's distinction is far from clear. It is plainly evident that he believes the material world to be adequately composed of the primary qualities, but it is not evident what status the secondary qualities have. Galileo does not deny that we sense primary qualities, and he does not deny that some bodies – those which are living animals with sense organs – have secondary qualities. He simply states that material bodies cannot be conceived without primary qualities, though they can be conceived without secondary qualities. This conceptual necessity implies that material things necessarily must actually have primary qualities, whereas secondary qualities are unnecessary and superfluous. The constancy of the primary qualities speaks for their abiding material reality.

Though Galileo wrote primarily as a physicist, he is usually believed to have been the great physicist he was because of his metaphysical

---

[1] Translated from *Il Saggiatore* by Edwin Arthur Burtt in *The Metaphysical Foundations of Modern Physical Science*, Revised Edition (London: Kegan Paul, Trench, Trubner & Co., Ltd., 1932), 75.
[2] *Ibid.*

convictions.[1] His study of Archimedes, Plato, and the Pythagoreans, and above all his own success in applying mathematics to physical problems evidently convinced him that the underlying reality of the material world is mathematical. If the basic units from which material things are made are geometrical atoms, then the real primary properties of these material things are those which can be treated mathematically. Even if we say cautiously that Galileo had a mathematical method, rather than a mathematical metaphysics, it is still not unfair to suggest that he found in his conception of material things those qualities which we call primary to be persistent because of his mathematical way of viewing the material world.

Gassendi also distinguishes between primary and secondary qualities. For Gassendi, all material things are made of conglomerations of atoms in the void. The primary properties of atoms are size, figure, weight, and a certain swiftness of motion; order and position are primary relations among the atoms. The primary qualities of the atoms are also those of the material things made out of them.[2] While all these properties are quantitative, Gassendi does not seem to have chosen them because they are amenable to mathematical representation, in this differing from Galileo. Gassendi places more stress upon the constancy of the primary qualities. He reasons that if atoms had colors and tastes and so on, there would not be such a variation of these qualities in material things during generation and corruption which are merely changes in the internal arrangements of the atoms making up things.[3] The sensible or secondary qualities, then, do not belong to material things but result from the primary qualities of atoms and their positioning in the structure of perceptible material things.

In its mechanical aspects Gassendi's theory of perception is similar in many ways to Descartes', but in its utilization of the void it presents an interesting contrast to the theory based in the Cartesian *plenum*. Gassendi believes that action can take place in the material world only through the motion and contact of material things; he denies both the efficacy of Scholastic internal occult qualities and action

---

[1] See Burtt, Edwin Arthur, *The Metaphysical Foundations of Modern Physical Science*, Revised Edition (London: Kegan Paul, Trench, Trubner & Co., Ltd., 1932); Crombie, A. C., "Galileo Galilei; A Philosophical Symbol", *Actes du VIIIᵉ Congrès International d'Histoire des Sciences* (Florence: 3–9 September 1956), 1089–1095; and Koyré, Alexandre, "Galileo and Plato," *Journal of the History of Ideas*, IV (1943), 400–428.

[2] Brett, G. S., *The Philosophy of Gassendi* (London: Macmillan and Co., Ltd., 1908), 63ff.; Thomas, P.-Félix, *La Philosophie de Gassendi* (Paris: Félix Alcan, 1889), 80ff.

[3] Gassendi, Pierre, *Dissertations en forme de paradoxes contre les aristotéliciens* (*Exercitationes Paradoxicæ adversus Aristoteleos*) *Livres I et II*, Texte latin établi, traduit et annoté par Bernard Rochot (Paris: J. Vrin, 1959), 474.

over a distance. Since in his system there is no all-pervading medium
through which motions might be conveyed – upon which the Cartesians
insist – it is obvious, he says, that for a thing to be perceived, something
material must travel from the thing to act upon and make it known to
the knower. He thus develops an Epicurean doctrine of emission.
Each material thing continually emits atoms arranged in patterns
similar to the structure of the thing. These groups of atoms travel in
straight lines with a uniform speed. If they strike the sense organs of a
human being before they are deflected or scattered, distinctive
motions are transferred from this contact along the nerves to the
brain where a material image – a plication, *image impresse* – is formed.
This causes the soul to have a sensation and an *image expresse* which
conforms to the thing known and represents it as it is objectively in
the soul. [1]

The sense organs do not respond only to the arrangements of the
emitted atoms, but each organ also responds to atoms of special types.
The sensation of heat arises from the impression upon the touch organ
of atoms distinguished by their primary qualities as heat atoms; there
are similarly special atoms which give rise to sensations of coldness.[2]
But it must be stressed that secondary qualities can be said to belong
to material things only in the sense that certain arrangements of primary qualities of atoms or groups of atoms uniformly give rise to certain
sensations if proper contact is made with sense organs. After such
contact is made, the mechanical aspects of perception proceed in
the body much as they do upon the Cartesian account. In no sense do
the atoms travel to the brain; their journey is done when they strike
the sense organs. Outside the body, the major difference is that on the
Cartesian account there is always a medium through which motions
can be transferred without the necessity of flying material atoms or
species.

Gassendi believes that the human soul has two parts, a sensitive
corporeal part and a reasonable incorporeal part. The sensitive part
is spread throughout the body, and though the sensorium is centered
in the brain, in some way the organs as well as the brain experience
sensations. This means that secondary or sensible qualities are properties of a material thing to the extent that the sensitive part of the soul is
material, though these secondary qualities do not picture the primary
qualities that cause them. The spiritual images or ideas which do

Thomas, P.-Félix, *La Philosophie de Gassendi* (Paris: Félix Alcan, 1889), 83ff., 122, 137.
[2] Brett, G. S., *The Philosophy of Gassendi* (London: Macmillan and Co., Ltd., 1908), 72ff.

represent the material things known arise in the incorporeal part of the soul. These images, Gassendi says, are always mixed with "quelque image de corporéité" because of the two-part nature of the soul in its union with the body.[1] While such an account may give rise to grave theological and metaphysical problems, it does not leave Gassendi with the problem – which we shall see the Cartesians facing – of how there can be an immaterial image of a material thing.

A final remark should be made about what might be called a Scholastic version of the Epicurean theory. In such a theory the flying atoms or species would be said to have sensible secondary as well as primary qualities. Some of the Cartesians, perhaps mistakenly, believed they had to combat such a theory. Gassendi, like the Cartesians, believes that the attribution of sensible qualities of material things by the Scholastics is one of their greatest mistakes. And as do the Cartesians, he offers his system with its careful distinction between primary and secondary qualities, and its notion of mechanical causality in the material world, as a reasonable alternative to the contradictory Scholastic account.

In the following chapters we shall more often speak of sensations and ideas than of secondary and primary qualities. In most cases it will be clear that sensations either are secondary qualities or represent secondary qualities, and that ideas represent primary qualities. This usage will suffice for the Cartesians. When groups of primary qualities are referred to as secondary qualities because they cause sensations, these passages will be well-marked. Deviations will also be apparent when we discuss non-Cartesians who believe that there can be sensations of primary qualities and ideas of secondary qualities. The distinction also often carries the implication that primary qualities are real properties of material things, whereas secondary qualities are not. Such categorization is implicit in much of the discussion which follows, though it should be remembered that for the Cartesians secondary qualities are real properties of spiritual things. And, as we have seen, some of the Scholastics believe that secondary qualities are real properties of material things, while, as we shall see, Foucher doubts that even primary qualities are real properties of material things.

---

[1] Mandon, L., *Étude sur le Syntagma Philosophicum de Gassendi* (Montpellier: Pierre Grollier, 1858), 76.

# CHAPTER II

# SIMON FOUCHER (1644-1696)

Simon Foucher is important in the history of modern philosophy as a sceptic who originated epistemological criticisms which were fatal to the Cartesian way of ideas. His method was that of the traditional sceptic: he assumed the principles of the system under analysis, and then reasoned to what he considered were contradictory conclusions. His arguments against the distinction between ideas and sensations were utilized by Bayle, Berkeley, and Hume. Any history of the Cartesian way of ideas, and any analysis of the representative theory of perception, must take into consideration the significant contribution of Simon Foucher.

Simon Foucher[1] was baptized in the parish of Notre-Dame of Dijon on 1 March 1644, the son of Nicolas Foucher, a merchant, and Anne Richot. He took orders at an early age at which time he was made honorary canon of the Sainte Chapelle of Dijon. His interest in classical letters and philosophy soon led him to Paris where he took a bachelor's degree at the Sorbonne in the faculty of theology. He spent the remainder of his life in Paris, dying on 27 April 1696, it is said, of overwork. He was buried in Saint-Nicolas-des-Champs.

Foucher spent his life in contact with some of the main philosophers and philosophical problems of his time. Baillet [2] says that in 1667 upon the return of Descartes' remains to Paris, Foucher was asked by

[1] Previous studies of Foucher are: Rabbe, Félix, *Étude philosophique, L'abbé Simon Foucher chanoine de la Sainte Chapelle de Dijon* (Paris: Didier et Cie., 1867); Gouhier, Henri, "La première polémique de Malebranche," *Revue d'histoire de la philosophie*, I (1927), 23-48, 168-191; Popkin, Richard H., "L'abbé Foucher et le problème des qualités premières". *Bulletin de la Société d'Étude du XVIIe Siècle*, No 33 (1957), 633-647; and in Popkin, Richard H., "The Sceptical Crisis and the Rise of Modern Philosophy, III," *Review of Metaphysics*, VII (1953-1954), 499-510. The biographical information which follows is taken primarily from these studies as well as from: Bouillier, Francisque, *Histoire de la philosophie cartésienne*, 2 volumes (Paris: Durand, 1854).

[2] Baillet, Adrien, *La Vie de Monsieur Descartes* (Paris: Daniel Horthemele, 1691). Part II, 439.

Rohault to deliver a funeral oration. If true, this suggests that the
young Foucher, not long arrived from the provinces, must have very
soon come into contact with the important Cartesians. Rabbe [1] believes that Foucher was at this time a Cartesian whose great promise
was awarded with the honor of giving the funeral oration. Gouhier, [2]
on the other hand, believes that Foucher must already have been an
Academic sceptic. Gouhier believes that Foucher was chosen because
he was a non-Cartesian who disliked Scholasticism and was favorable
to Descartes' method of doubt. Foucher could thus be counted on
to give a relatively nonpartisan account of Descartes as a great and
pious man. Gouhier bases his speculations upon Foucher's statement
that he had begun arguments with Rohault in 1667 concerning
knowledge of the world of extension, which suggests he was not a
Cartesian then. It is also improbable that he left the Jesuit college
in Dijon as a Cartesian. There is no record of Foucher's giving the
oration and one can wonder if he were ever asked, and if so, if he ever
prepared it. Foucher was somewhat vain about his writing, and though
we have no copies of his first *Dissertations sur la recherche de la verité, ou
sur la logique des academiciens* of 1673, [3] he refers to them several times.
He published two long poems and left a drama in manuscript. [4] Since
he did believe that Descartes was a great man, it seems unlikely that
if he had been asked to give the oration or had prepared it he would
not have left a reference to it. Neither Clerselier nor Rohault mention
it. All of this is negative evidence, however, and from Baillet's simple
statement that Foucher was asked it is probably just as out of place to
suggest that he was not as to speculate about why he was. It is at least
very probable that Foucher attended Rohault's weekly lectures on
Cartesianism in 1667 and 1668; Foucher could easily have raised his
objections from the floor and not have been an intimate of Rohault at
all.

In Paris, Foucher was the chaplain of some religious men who lived
on rue Saint-Denis. Huet knew Foucher and though he had respect for
him, did not feel that he was a very good historian, claiming that
Foucher hardly knew the names of Carneades and Arcesilas, and that

---

[1] Rabbe, *op. cit.*, 5.

[2] Gouhier, *op. cit.*, 31ff.

[3] Foucher, Simon, *Dissertations sur la recherche de la verité, ou sur la logique des academiciens* (Dijon: publisher unknown, 1673). Hereafter referred to as *Logique*.

[4] Foucher, Simon, *Sur la mort de la reine* (Paris: publisher unknown, 1666); Foucher, Simon, *De la Sagesse des anciens, où l'on fait voir que les principales maximes de leur morale ne sont pas contraires au christianisme* (Paris: Dezailliers, 1682). The drama is entitled *L'Empereur Léonce.*

he knew less of Pyrrhonism. At one time Huet tried to get Foucher a position with Charles de Sainte-Maure, Duke of Montausier and tutor to the Dauphine, but after a long visit and dinner during which Huet says Foucher fought with everyone and tried continually to talk of things unsuitable to the place and the people present, the Duke did not even wish to hear Foucher's name spoken again.[1] Ménage thought Foucher a good historian,[2] though Huet's opinion is probably more accurate.

Leibniz [3] was in Paris on a diplomatic mission during the years 1672–1676. There he met Lantin and La Mare, Conseillers to Parlement from Dijon. Foucher was Lantin's friend and it was probably through Lantin that he met Leibniz. In the later correspondence between Foucher and Leibniz, Lantin is often mentioned. Leibniz corresponded with Foucher for two reasons. First, he valued his criticisms and was stimulated by his ingenious arguments. Second, Foucher was active in trying to get Leibniz admitted to the Académie des Sciences. Foucher was in contact with Thevenot, was a friend of Jean-Baptiste Du Hamel who was working on a history of the Académie, and knew Gallois who was responsible for Leibniz's contributions appearing in the *Mémoires de l'Académie*. Foucher and Leibniz exchanged letters from 1676 to 1695, culminating in the publication of extracts in the *Journal des Sçavans* in 1692–1696 [4] which include the

[1] Letter of Huet to Nicaise (25 juillet 1697) in: Cousin, Victor, *Fragments philosophiques pour faire suite aux cours de l'histoire de la philosophie*, 4 volumes (Paris: Ladrange and Didier, 1847). III, 153–154. Quoted by Rabbe, *op. cit.*, X.

[2] Menage, Gilles. *Menagiana, ou les bons mots et remarques critiques, historiques, morales & d'érudition, de Monsieur Menage, recueilles par ses amis*. Nouvelle édition. Paris: Veuve Delaulne, 1729. Menage says Foucher "sçait parfaitement l'histoire des philosophes" and ranks him side by side with Huet as an historian. 358ff.

[3] Barber, W. H., *Leibniz in France from Arnauld to Voltaire, A Study in French Reactions to Leibnizianism, 1670–1760* (Oxford: Clarendon Press, 1955), 4ff.

[4] "Extrait d'une lettre de Monsr. de Leibniz à Mr. Foucher chanoine de Dijon, sur quelques axiomes de philosophie," *Journal des sçavans* (Amsterdam), XX (2 juin 1692), 365–369.

"Extrait d'une lettre de M. Foucher chanoine de Dijon, pour repondre à M. de Leibniz sur quelques axiomes de philosophie," *Journal des sçavans* (Amsterdam), XXI (16 mars 1693), 182–186.

"Reponse de Mr. de Leibniz à l'extrait de la lettre de Mr. Foucher chanoine de Dijon, inserée dans le journal du 16 mars 1693," *Journal des sçavans* (Amsterdam), XXI (3 aoust 1693), 527–529.

"Sistême nouveau de la nature & de la communication des substances, aussi bien que de l'union qu'il y a entre l'ame & le corps. Par M.D.L.," *Journal des sçavans* (Amsterdam), XXXII (27 juin 1695), 444–454, (4 juillet 1695), 455–462.

"Réponse de M. S. F. à M. de L. B. Z. sur son nouveau sisteme de la communication des substances, proposé dans les journaux de 27 juin & du 4 juillet 1695," *Journal des sçavans* (Amsterdam), XXXII (12 septembre 1695), 639–645.

"Eclaircissement du nouveau systeme de la communication des substances, pour servir de reponse à ce qui en a été dit dans le journal du 12 sept. 1695," *Journal des sçavans* (Amsterdam), XXIV (2 avril 1696), 255–258, (9 avril 1696), 259–263.

first public expression and criticism of Leibniz's theory of monads and pre-established harmony.

Foucher's first published work was a long poem upon the death of Anne of Austria, published in Paris in 1666.[1] Nearly every verse is inspired by a Latin quotation which is given in the margin. *Cupio dissolvi & esse cum Christo* accompanies the penetrating lines:

> Son corps la captivoit, une divine flâme
>     En sçait rompre les nœuds,
> Ces indignes climats étoient pour sa grande Ame
>     Un sejour ennuyeux.[2]

One might speculate about the young canon's literary ambitions. Perhaps he heard of Anne's death while still in Dijon, and wrote the poem. Receiving praise in Dijon, the young poet may have set off for Paris, manuscript in hand, with high hopes for the future. It is an intriguing picture, though highly speculative.

In 1672 Foucher published an 18 page letter entitled *Nouvelle façon d'hygrometres*[3] in which he describes several instruments for measuring the humidity of the air. This work was reprinted in 1686 [4] along with five further letters on the same subject. Foucher's interest in experimental physics was probably fostered by Rohault's lectures.

In 1673 Foucher had a small number of copies of his *Dissertations sur la recherche de la verité, ou sur la logique des academiciens* printed in Dijon.[5] He distributed it personally; it was not put up for sale. He remarked to Leibniz (probably in 1685) that even he had no more copies.[6] There are none available today, but the essence of this work is incorporated into Foucher's other *Dissertations*.[7] Foucher no doubt distributed his *Logique* of 1673 among the philosophers in Paris; in it he speaks of the need for workers in "la recherche de la vérité." Considering the similarity of the titles (though it is not an uncommon title), Foucher perhaps had some grounds for thinking that Malebranche's *Recherche de la vérité* of 1674 was in response to the call in the *Logique* of

---

[1] Foucher, Simon, *Sur la mort de la reine* (Paris: publisher unknown, 1666).

[2] *Ibid.*, 3.

[3] Foucher, Simon, *Nouvelle façon d'hygrometres* (place and publisher unknown, 1672).

[4] Foucher, Simon, *Traité des hygrometres ou machines pour mesurer la secheresse et l'humidité de l'air* (Paris, Estienne Michallet, 1686).

[5] Foucher, Simon, *Dissertations sur la recherche de la verité, ou sur la logique des academiciens* (Dijon: publisher unknown, 1673).

[6] Letter of Foucher to Leibniz (1685?) in: *Die Philosophischen Schriften von Gottfried Wilhelm Leibniz*, Herausgegeben von C. J. Gerhardt, (Berlin: Weidmannsche, 1875). "Briefwechsel zwischen Leibniz und Foucher," I, 378–379.

[7] *Ibid.*, Foucher to Leibniz (Paris, 8 decembre 1684), 376–378.

1673. He seems to believe in his *Critique de la Recherche de la verité* of 1675 that the *Logique* could not have been unknown to Malebranche. But, if Foucher truly believed that Malebranche had written at least partially from the inspiration of the *Logique*, one wonders just how close Foucher's contact with the philosophic world of Paris was. Malebranche spent several years writing the *Recherche*. The first volume was finished in 1673 and the manuscript was in circulation;[1] there must have been some gossip about the work Malebranche was doing. It seems likely that many knew that the author of the *Recherche* was Malebranche and that a second volume was nearly ready for the press. Malebranche at least, did not feel it necessary to put a volume number on the work published in 1674. In any event, it is clear that for lack of intelligence of one kind or another Foucher took the 1674 volume of the *Recherche* as a complete work and criticized it as such. That a more substantial excuse for his doing this than the speculation that he frequented the wrong cafes is given in Chapter IV. If he did not know beforehand about the first volume of the *Recherche*, he certainly had prior warning of the second of 1675. Ouvrard reports that Foucher could hardly wait for it to appear and that he was unapproachable for some time after it did.[2] Foucher's *Réponse pour la Critique à la Preface du second volume de la Recherche de la verité* appeared in 1676.[3] Malebrache removed the offensive preface in the fourth edition of the *Recherche* in 1678, so Foucher removed his preface in the second edition of the *Réponse* of 1679; he still felt, however, that the *Réponse* deserved a second printing.

In 1675 also appeared Desgabets' *Critique de la Critique de la Recherche de la vérité*.[4] Foucher replied to Desgabets in 1676 in his *Nouvelle dissertation*,[5] and again in his *Dissertation … contenant l'apologie des académiciens* of 1687.[6] Finally in 1693 appeared Foucher's last work,

[1] Malebranche, Nicolas, *De la Recherche de la vérité où l'on traite de la nature de l'esprit de l'homme, et de l'usage qu'il en doit faire pour éviter l'erreur des sciences*, Introduction et Texte Établi par Geneviève Lewis, 3 volumes (Paris: J. Vrin, 1945), I, Préface, II.

[2] Letter of Ouvrard to Nicaise (24 septembre 1675) in: Cousin, Victor, *Fragments Philosophiques pour faire suite aux cours de l'histoire de la philosophie*, 4 volumes (Paris: Ladrange and Didier, 1847), III, 154–155. Quoted by Rabbe, *op. cit.*, 7–8.

[3] Foucher, Simon, *Réponse pour la Critique à la Preface du second volume de la Recherche de la verité, où l'on examine le sentiment de M. Descartes touchant les idées, avec plusieurs remarques pour les sciences* (Paris: Charles Angot, 1676).

[4] Desgabets, Robert, *Critique de la Critique de la Recherche de la vérité, où l'on découvre le chemin qui conduit aux connoissances solides. Pour servir de réponse à la Lettre d'un académicien.* (Paris: Jean Du Puis, 1675).

[5] Foucher, Simon, *Nouvelle dissertation sur la recherche de la vérité, contenant la Reponse a la Critique de la Critique de la Recherche de la verité, où l'on découvre les erreurs de dogmatistes, tant anciens que nouveaux, avec une discution particuliere du grand principe des cartesiens* (Paris: Robert de la Caille, 1679). (The included *Reponse* is dated 23 mai 1676.)

[6] Foucher, Simon, *Dissertation sur la recherche de la verité, contenant l'apologie des academiciens,*

*Dissertation . . . contenant l'histoire des académiciens,*[1] in four parts incorporating the essence of all the *Dissertations* which had gone before plus some new material. There is a great deal of repetition in Foucher's critiques, responses, and dissertations.

Foucher also wrote two works on moral philosophy, one in verse, to show that the pagan philosophers have principles similar to Christian ones.[2]

Having examined Foucher's life and works, let us now consider his Academic scepticism and his positive position. Foucher is known as the restorer of the Academic philosophy.[3] He says that he is an Academic in the manner of Plato, not that he is a Platonist, but that he follows the Platonic method of philosophizing.[4] By this he seems to mean primarily that he, and the other Academics, reject the senses as a source of knowledge, depending only on reason. And also, that all Academic philosophy is founded in Socratic ignorance; the Academic philosopher knows little more or less than anyone else, except that he knows his own ignorance.

Foucher's major *Dissertations* were written to give an exposition of the Academic philosophy. They are, in turn, *La logique des academiciens* (1673), *L'apologie des academiciens* (1687), and *L'histoire des academiciens* (1693). His sources for these works are Cicero, Plutarch, Sextus Empiricus, Diogenes Laertius, and Augustine.[5] The following is a short exposition of Foucher's positive views as he has adapted them from the Academic philosophers. There is little attempt here to question his interpretations, beyond remarking that they are somewhat free, perhaps because one of his intents was to show that Academic principles are most fitted to lead one to Christianity.

A very short outline can be given of the principle Academics. Foucher paraphrases their view as follows:

*Socrates:*   *Je sçais que je ne sçais pas.*
*Arcesilas:*   Je ne sçais pas même que je sçais que je ne sçais pas.

*où l'on fait voir que leur maniere de philosopher est la plus utile pour la religion, & la plus conforme au bon sens, pour servir de Réponse à la Critique de la Critique, &c. avec plusieurs remarques sur les erreurs des sens & sur l'origine de la philosophie de Monsieur Descartes* (Paris: Estienne Michallet, 1687). Hereafter referred to as *Apologie.*
[1] Foucher, Simon, *Dissertations sur la recherche de la recherche de la verité, contenant l'histoire et les principes de la philosophie des academiciens. Avec plusieurs réflexions sur les sentimens de M. Descartes* (Paris: Jean Anisson, 1693). Hereafter referred to as *Histoire.*
[2] *De la Sagesse des anciens, où l'on fait voir que les principales maximes de leur morale ne sont pas contraires au christianisme* (Paris: Dezailliers, 1682); *Lettre sur la morale de Confucius, philosophe de la Chine* (Paris: Daniel Horthemels, 1688).
[3] Letter of Leibniz to Nicaise (1697) quoted in Rabbe, *op. cit.,* VIII.
[4] Letter of Foucher to Leibniz (Paris, 3 mai 1687), Gerhardt, *op. cit.,* 388–389.
[5] *Histoire,* 10.

*Carneades:*  Je doute si je sçais que je ne sçais rien.
  *Philo:*  Je sçais peu de chose & j'en ignore beaucoup.
*Antiochus:*  Je sçais plusieurs choses & j'en ignore plusieurs.[1]

After Socrates on principle, Foucher agrees most with Antiochus and Philo.[2] He admits that Arcesilas ended as a Pyrrhonist, but like Carneades he began in Socratic ignorance. But even the Pyrrhonians cannot actually be said to be opposed to the Academic dictum to search for the truth, for they make no dogmatic assertions at all.[3] Among the church fathers, Augustine can be counted as "Chef d'Academie." [4] He was really for, not against them, and he worked to show that Academic principles can be accommodated to those of Christendom.[5] Lactanius did the same, and further stressed that knowledge cannot be based on probabilities. With this Foucher is in full agreement. Descartes is an Academic in that he correctly commences in metaphysics by rejecting all propositions which can be doubted, but unfortunately he does not abide by this rule and so falls into dogmatism.[6]

Foucher is a sceptic, but in a limited sense. He distinguishes Academic beliefs from two extremes of dogmatism, that which claims that everything can be known and that which claims that nothing can be known.

C'est ainsi que les Academiciens combatoient les prejugez des Dogmatistes, & tachoient de les reduire dans un doute raisonnable: non pas pour les y arrêter entierement; mais au contraire pour les obliger d'en sortir de maniere à n'y rentrer jamais. Il est vray que les Academiciens doivent douter d'une tres-grande quantité des choses, mais c'est parce que ces choses sont douteuses, & il se trouve neamoins que le sprincipales veritez leur sont connuës, de sorte que leurs doutes regardent seulement les matieres de sciences, & les propositions dogmatiques que l'on pourroit faire sur les sujets de pure speculation humaine.[7]

Foucher believes that we do have some certain knowledge, but doubts that we have or can have knowledge of the essences of external things. Let us begin, then, with what the Academic knows for certain.

Philosophy should begin with an examination of first principles.[8]

---

[1] *Apologie*, 31–32.
[2] *Ibid.*, 83.
[3] *Ibid.*, 25.
[4] *Histoire*, 67.
[5] *Apologie*, 31, 38.
[6] *Ibid.*, 31.
[7] *Ibid.*, [viii] – [ix].
[8] *Histoire*, 80.

The first principle, "la grande maxime," of the Academics is that "ils ne reconnoissent que la verité évidente pour regle, & à son défaut la foi, *in fide & veritate*." [1] It is most reasonable to follow evident truths in matters of knowledge, the laws of one's country in matters of life, and faith in matters of religion. Among first principles that are certainly known are five which Foucher gives as the laws of the Academic philosophers:

(1) *Ne se conduire que par Demonstration en matiere de Philosophie.*
(2) *Ne point agiter les questions que nous voions bien ne pouvoir decider.*
(3) *Avoüer que l'on ne sçait pas, ce que l'on ignore effectivement.*
(4) *Distinguer les choses que l'on sçait de celles que l'on ne sçait pas.*
(5) *Chercher toûjours des connoissances nouvelles.*[2]

He also stresses three important axioms:

(1) *Judicium veritatis non est in sensibus.*
(2) *Non opinaturum esse sapientem.*
(3) *Verba non dant conceptus, sed supponent.*[3]

Socratic ignorance and reasonable doubt, then, are far from leading the Academic philosopher to deny that we have knowledge. These five laws and three axioms are offered, like the first "grande maxime," as self-evident truths. The fifth law expressly states that the business of a philosopher is to search after truth, "chercher la verité n'est autre chose que philosopher." [4] Thus, "les Academiciens sont plus éloignez des prejugez que les autres Philosophes, puis qu'ils dêcident moins & qu'ils ne se hazardent pas à suive de simples vray-semblances." [5]

The three axioms, like the truths of mathematics, Foucher calls dogmas of the Academics. The first means that knowledge of the essences of things cannot be gained from sense experience. The second does not deny that in the actions of life we must often act by opinion, but this can go easily with suspense of judgment concerning the truth. [6] The third simply means that words are the arbitrary signs of the ideas they excite, and that we must have these ideas before words can be applied to them. Simple ideas come only through experience, but complex ideas can be constructed by putting together simple ideas or the words which are signs of them. Foucher says that this means that

---

[1] *Apologie*, 56.
[2] *Ibid.*, 5–8, 44–45.
[3] *Ibid.*, 88, 102, 107; Letter of Foucher to Leibniz (Paris, aoust 1692), Gerhardt, *op. cit.*, 406–409.
[4] *Apologie*, 47; *Histoire*, 217.
[5] *Apologie*, 12.
[6] *Ibid.*, 102–103.

there are two kinds of logic necessary:

L'une qui doit servir à nous acquerir les idées que nous n'avons pas, ou à éclaircir celles que nous avons confuses. L'autre à exposer & décrire les idées que nous avons afin de découvrir aux autres les veritez que nous connoissons dés-jà. L'une est proprement la recherche de la verité, & l'autre retient plus proprement le nom de Logique, concernant le discours & l'arrangement des propositions.[1]

The first is the more important; it is best pursued with Academic principles. The second, which is harmful without the first, is most highly developed by the Peripatetics.

In metaphysics, then, the Academics recognize such truths as the existence of a good and just God, and of two sorts of being, one created, the other uncreated. In morals, such truths as that the goods of fortune are not capable of rendering us happy, and that one should not contradict one's self, nor suppose what is in question, nor conduct oneself by prejudices in matters of knowledge, and that we are obliged to make good use of our reason. The major dogma, again, is that evident reason is necessary in matters of knowledge, with the concomitant reasonable conclusions that probabilities are sufficient for the particular actions of life and for the establishment of historical facts, and that reason should be silenced in matters of religion.[2] One must restrict reasonable doubt in order to live, but it is better to doubt too much than to doubt too little in the search for knowledge.[3]

We have seen the first principles; we must now inquire into the search for truth. What we are looking for when we search for the truth is a way to determine if our judgments are true, that is, the goal of philosophy is to learn how to avoid error in judgments.[4] This means that we must find a criterion of truth. After the criterion is found, we want to use it to discover knowledge of the essences of external things, and then a necessary order in that knowledge.[5] Let us proceed in order.

There are good signs that we shall be able to find the criterion. We do know some truths, for example, mathematical truths, so we

---

[1] *Ibid.*, 108. Menage, *op. cit.*, 360–361, reports similar comments by Foucher on the subject of two logics. Academic logic "enseigne à découvrir la verité, & ... à bien penétrer les principes." Such a logic is possible, Foucher says, "car après tout, les idées composent les paroles & le langage de l'esprit." Thus, "il est nécessaire de travailler à une *Grammaire des Idees.*"

[2] *Apologie*, 36, 16.
[3] *Histoire*, 140.
[4] *Apologie*, 72.
[5] *Ibid.*, 129.

know what truth is in general. Foucher says this saves us from having to seek a criterion for our criterion, and so on. No one has ever doubted that 2 plus 2 equals 4 is necessarily true, or that 2 plus 2 equals 5 is necessarily false; mathematical truths are true, even if they exist only in our minds.[1] The careful way this is put actually leads us to two criteria. All the truths we have mentioned above are self-evidently certain; they have the evidence of reason. The evidence of such self-evident principles is such that only a madman would not accept them.[2] We are psychologically incapable of doubting them, and for good reason; the general and evident truths which the Academics accept "sont écrites & imprimées dans tous les esprits." [3] They constitute the natural, eternal light from God and are accepted by all men of good sense. They are recognizable in themselves, also, and in this we have a second criterion of truth. This is that a proposition is true if it is inconceivable that its contradictory could be true. Hence, for the discovery of truths beyond these which are immediately self-evident, the principle of contradiction is necessary.[4]

There is a third criterion of truth which even the Pyrrhonians recognize. All the knowledge we have of pain, pleasure, sweetness, bitterness, light, darkness, red, green, heat, cold, and the other sensible qualities is not denied to be true by the Academics. With the Pyrrhonians they take "pour leur *Criterium*, la perception ou façon-d'être connuë par elle-même." These interior things are perfectly comprehensible as they are known in themselves "par conscience." No one denies that they are what they are.[5]

Do we, then, have among these three criteria of truth a criterion for determining the truth of propositions about the essences of external things? Foucher's caution about mathematical truths shows us that we do not. He says that the evidence we have that 2 plus 2 equals 4 is such that the mind could not desire anything more evident and invariable; however, for all we know such truth may be only for propositions in the mind and not apply to judgments about the external world.[6] We can easily prove that we have many truths which are certain because our reason leads infallibly to necessary truths. If it did not, there would be no constant truths. However, we do have constant

---

[1] *Histoire*, 132–133.
[2] *Ibid.*, 120.
[3] *Apologie*, 75.
[4] *Histoire*, 140, 199.
[5] *Apologie*, 91–93.
[6] *Histoire*, 141.

truths, hence our reason must be trustworthy. If this is not enough, one need only consider that he cannot will such truths to be otherwise.[1] But when we judge that these truths apply to the external world, we add something the judgment and for this new judgment we have no criterion of truth. This is apparent in Foucher's answer to the objection that mathematical truths are contested:

On ne les conteste que pour les choses qui sont hors de nostre esprit & à *parte rei*, mais pour ce qui regarde la conception de ces veritez, elle est incontestable. Il est certain que les deux costez d'un triangle pris ensemble, composent un ligne plus grande que le troisiéme de ces costez separement, soit qu'il y ait des lignes & des triangles hors de nous, soit qu'il n'y en ait point, d'ailleurs les Academiciens ne pretendoient pas trouver, en matiere de Philosophie, des veritez plus certenes que celle de Geometrie, & je declare que je m'en contenterois.[2]

The third criterion, that of sensible knowledge, offers at least a purchase on the external world. Foucher is quite explicit in saying that we cannot know the natures of external things, either by the internal ideas discussed above or by the senses:

nos sens ne sçauroient être les juges de la verité des choses qui sont hors de nous; parce que nous ne connoissons point ces choses en *elles-mêmes*. Du moins par les sens nous n'en connoissons que les apparences & nous ne sçaurions sçavoir si ces apparences nous les representant telles qu'elles sont, parce que nous ne sçauriens les comparer avec les realitez de ces choses que nous ne concevons pas, il en est de même que si nous ne pouvions voir l'original de quelques portraits; il nous seroit impossible de juger des défauts de ces portraits ne les pouvant comparer avec leurs originaux.

He continues that we do not have direct knowledge of external things through the senses,

car si ces choses nous estoient ainsi connuës, elles seroient en nous, & ne seroient pas hors de nous, ce qui seroit contradictoire. En effet la connoissance étant une action immanente, il faut que le terme de cette action soit dans la faculté ou substance qui connoît, autrement la connoissance seroit une action au dehors ce qui ne se peut; car ce seroit connoissance & ce ne seroit pas connoissance.[3]

It is impossible to know the essences of external things, for by our nature we can only know things in our minds. Aristotle and the other ancient philosophers recognized this, Foucher says, and that is why they were obliged to discuss ideas or phantoms in conceiving of exterior things. It is even more apparent that what we sense immediately

---

[1] *Ibid.*, 196–198.
[2] *Apologie.* 154.
[3] *Ibid.*, 86–87.

are only phenomenal appearances which are in the substance of our mind. Plato, Sextus Empiricus, Descartes, Rohault, Arnauld, Nicole, and Desgabets all agree in this with Foucher and the Academics.[1]

Even though we cannot know external things in themselves by the senses, we can know that they exist as the causes of our sensations. And we can distinguish them from one another if they (1) cause some modification in us (2) which we can know and (3) which is more related to one particular external thing than to any other.

Cela posé, je dis qu'il est impossible de connoître les choses exterieures en elles-mêmes; c'est à dire de premiere veuë, d'où il s'ensuit manifestement que la premiere chose que je connois par les sens sont les resultats de l'action des objets exterieurs, & non pas ces mêmes objets ou leurs realitez, parce que ces realitez estant hors de nous, ne sçauroient être connuës immediatement en elles mêmes, étant impossible que nôtre ame sorte d'elle-même pour aller dans ces objets, & que ces objets se rendent presens à nôtre ame, à moins que de luy devenir interieurs, auquel cas, ils deviendroient des façons-d'être de nôtre ame, & ne seroient pas connus tels qu'ils seroient étant entrez en nous. Tant il est vray que la connoissance est immanente, & n'embrasse rien d'exterieur immediatement.[2]

Since ideas are also "façons-d'être" of our soul, it is manifest that they also do not give us direct knowledge of external things in themselves, nor any knowledge of their natures at all. It "est impossible de concevoir ces choses en elles-mêmes vû qu'elles sont hors de nous." [3] What we know "ne sont que des façons-d'être ou des modifications de nôtre propre substance." Finally, "il est impossible que les choses soient veritablement tout ce qu'elles paroissent être." [4] Foucher's development of this consequence against Malebranche is treated in Chapter IV.

Therefore, though Foucher does have knowledge, he has no criterion for determining if these truths in the mind also apply to the external world. That such a criterion could ever be found seems to be denied by the very conditions of knowing; about external things we seem condemned to know no more than that they exist as causes of our diverse sensations. Nevertheless, Foucher says it is the task of the philosopher to continue the search.

Despite the fact that we cannot have certain knowledge of external things, we can have a kind of "connoissances artificielles" which we

[1] *Ibid.*, 88.
[2] *Ibid.*, 90–91.
[3] *Ibid.*, 95.
[4] *Ibid.*, 100.

ourselves have formed from sense experience.[1] This artificial knowledge might be true, and it certainly is useful. Foucher appeals to it in answer to the objection that Academic exactitude is useless for no one has yet found any truth in natural philosophy. Just as we cannot be certain that it is impossible to find, Foucher says, it is also not certain that no one has yet found it. Academic principles have had their part in the new science of the 17th century, in the making of such discoveries as telescopes, microscopes, algebra, the laws of the equilibrium of liquids, and the art of navigation. Granted that these discoveries are less than certain knowledge, they were made only by conformity to rules very similar to those of the Academics. Foucher believes that Academic logic is much wider spread than many people think.[2] Mathematical knowledge in particular is quite useful, for with nothing but mathematics we can "expliquer toute la Physique, parce que l'Univers estant une grande Machine, on en peut reduire tous les mouvemens & tous le ressorts aux lois de la Mechanique, *in pondere, numero, & mensura*." [3] But only a dogmatic Cartesian would insist that this speculation about the causes of our sensations is certain knowledge. What the Academics say is that these mathematical applications to physics are of the highest probability. It is not infallible knowledge, but neither is it confused nor subject to ordinary doubt.

Ce n'est pas qu'ils crûssent que nous pouvons juger des choses exterieures, en les comparant avec les idées que nous en avons, car il faudroit pour cela connoistre ces choses en elles-mêmes & immediatement; auquel cas nous n'aurions pas besoin d'idées pour les representer: mais c'est que nous pouvons sçavoir ce qu'il nous est permis d'attribuer à ces choses & ce qu'on ne leur doit point attribuer. Quoy que nous ne puissions connoistre immediatement les triangles qui sont hors de nous, nous pouvons neanmoins estre assurez, que s'il y en a, leurs angles ne valent que deux droits: je veux que nostre conclusion en cela, ne soit qu'hypotetique, neanmoins elle est certene.[4]

That is, as mathematics it is certain knowledge; as physics it is hypothetical. Foucher is certainly correct that if there are triangles in the external world, they have the properties of triangles. But it is easy to understand how such hypothetical certainty is unsatisfactory to the dogmatist. At the peak of Foucher's investigations of the external world he still does not know whether or not it contains a triangle.

This does not mean that Foucher is in favor of depending upon probability in philosophy. This is the major defect of dogmatic philoso-

[1] *Ibid.*, 87.
[2] *Ibid.*, 152, 156.
[3] *Ibid.*, 148–149.
[4] *Ibid.*, 145–146.

phers, that they become too enamored of their prejudices. Even the Academics will admit that some of their principles are probable, but it is a gross mistake to take probabilities as certain truths; a true system of knowledge cannot be built upon probabilities.[1]

Foucher goes on to derive more truths from his principles than anyone might think possible. They parallel those of the Cartesian system, and while there is an element of grotesque virtuosity in the performance, it is undoubtedly serious. If from nothing else, this is evident from the fact that a careful examination shows that all these truths are about existence, but not about essences. First of all, our soul is known before all other things. This is because we know immediately only modifications of our soul, so if we know anything, we know our soul. This knowledge, however, is only of the soul's properties and not of its essence. The soul is a thinking being, but we do not know what this being is. However, the Academics can easily prove the spirituality and unity of the soul; that is, there must be an indivisible subject of all our thoughts, sensations, and judgments. It would be impossible to construct a thinking being from insensible and separable parts, therefore the soul is a spiritual unity. Plotinus very well pointed out that for the comprehension of the diversity of sensation, there must be a unitary point – the soul – of comparison. From the unity and indivisibility of the soul immediately follows its immortality, for what cannot be broken up into parts is immortal. Foucher admits that the various modifications of the soul succeed one another and pass away, but their reality is nothing more than the substance they inhere in which remains. Incidentally, Foucher proves that we cannot know the essence of matter. If we knew matter immediately, then, as Plato says, we could not prove the immortality of the soul nor the existence of God.[2] But we have just proved the immortality of the soul and will prove the existence of God in the next paragraph. By not claiming that the essence of matter is extension, however, let it be noted that the Academics can admit with little embarrassment the real interaction of minds and bodies which everyone experiences taking place. That no one has been able to explain this interaction might be evidence that the essences of mind and matter are not yet known.[3]

The Academic demonstration of the existence of God depends upon the necessity of a Creator of substance. In particular, all extension

---

[1] *Ibid.*, 12–13.
[2] *Ibid.*, 121–130.
[3] *Histoire*, 187–188.

presupposes thought; all the movement, figure, union, generation, corruption, composition, and dissolution of bodies which cause our sensations cannot exist without the prior thought of an Understanding which gives it being. The Academics, along with Plato, recognize this. Hence, the existence and reality of substance in the universe is proof of the existence of God. A unique eternal Understanding is implied, hence the unity of God is proved. And, since thought is required for existence, the continual production of created things is proved, for they would cease to exist if God ceased to conceive them. The freedom of man and the providence of God easily follow on Academic principles from the recognition that we can suspend our judgment on doubtful questions. And though we do not know the essences of external things, God does. [1] Finally, Academic principles are most fitted to lead one to Christianity, for they say to search for the truth; it is a most reasonable truth to accept Divine Faith.

Since the *Dissertations* are meant in part to be examinations of Descartes' principles, it will be well to complete this chapter by giving Foucher's evaluation. We have just seen some similarities and differences between their systems. They agree that the senses are not a source of knowledge of essences. The similarity between Foucher's five Academic rules and Descartes' rules of method is quite apparent. Foucher says it is obvious why the Academics and the Cartesians agree in method; Descartes took his rules from the Academics.[2] Where Descartes went wrong, Foucher says, is in following the first Academic law while failing to follow the third. He should not have affirmed "que tout ce qui est clairement enfermé dans nos idées, est contenu dans les choses que ces idées nous represent." Foucher does not understand "comment nos façons-d'être nous peuvent representer des choses differentes de nous-mêmes." In the Cartesian system, Foucher says,

il faut premierement sçavoir si nos façons-d'être nous peuvent representer quelque chose de different de nous-mêmes, & quoy qu'on appelle les façons-d'être des idées, il ne n'ensuit pas pour cela qu'elles soient representatives des choses exterieures.[3]

Descartes certainly begs the question here.[4] We cannot know if ideas are similar to things, but even more,

de vouloir que des choses ou idées qui n'ont ni étenduës, ni figures, representent neamoins de certaines étenduës determinées & de certaines figures!

---

[1] *Apologie*, 131–132, 135, 137, 140–141, 147.
[2] *Histoire*, 187.
[3] *Apologie*, 111–112.
[4] *Histoire*, 76.

pour moy je pense que si cela n'est absurde & impossible du moins cela n'est pas si évident qu'on n'en puisse douter.[1]

Foucher's development of these objections against Malebranche is given in Chapter IV.

The *cogito* is obviously not the first principle, since we must know that everything that thinks also exists, and that everything must either be or not be to establish the *cogito*.[2] Foucher does agree with Descartes that our proper being consists in thought, [3] but, as we have seen, by this he does not mean that we know the essence of the thinking being, only that it has properties which are thoughts. The real dogmatism of Descartes comes in his assertion that we know the essences of mind and body. Because of this claim, Foucher says, Descartes cannot admit the real interaction between mind and body that Foucher can by admitting that he does not know their essences. Foucher also differs with Descartes on the idea of infinity and infinite divisibility, and, as has been shown, in his proof of the existence of God.[4]

[1] *Apologie*, 113.
[2] *Histoire*, 92.
[3] *Apologie*, 85.
[4] *Histoire*, 187–188.

# CHAPTER III

# LATE 17TH CENTURY CARTESIAN METAPHYSICS AND CRITICISMS OF IT

We are now ready to characterize the Cartesian system. The basic metaphysical position established will be considered as the one to which orthodox Cartesians attempt to adhere. Malebranche, for example, as he himself stresses, is not an orthodox Cartesian. Rohault, La Forge, Régis, Le Grand, and in most respects Desgabets and Arnauld are or attempt to be orthodox Cartesians.

The last grand expositor of the Cartesian philosophy was Antoine Le Grand who in 1694 published *An Entire Body of Philosophy*. The characterization of the late 17th Century Cartesian metaphysical system given below follows Le Grand's exposition more closely than others, but it also incorporates elements from those of Malebranche, Desgabets, La Forge, Rohault, Régis and Arnauld.[1] None of the Cartesians used as sources professed a system of exactly the sort this characterization pictures, nor is it implied here that they did. The guide and rationale for drawing from them such a model Cartesianism is the polemical writing of Simon Foucher.[2] His series of attacks upon

---

[1] Le Grand, Antoine. *An Entire Body of Philosophy According to the Principles of the Famous Renate des Cartes.* (London: Roycroft, 1694).

Malebranche, Nicolas. *De la recherche de la vérité où l'on traite de la nature de l'esprit de l'homme, et de l'usage qu'il en doit faire pour éviter l'erreur des sciences.* In *Oeuvres complètes.* 20 volumes. Direction: André Robinet. (Paris: J. Vrin, 1958–). I & II.

Desgabets, Robert. *Critique de la Critique de la Recherche de la vérité, où l'on découvre le chemin qui conduit aux connoissances solides. Pour servir de réponse à la Lettre d'un académicien.* (Paris: du Puis, 1675).

Desgabets, Robert. *Supplément à la philosophie de M. Descartes.* Selections in Lemaire, Paul. *Le Cartésianisme chez les Bénédictins. Dom Robert Desgabets son système, son influence et son école, d'après plusieurs manuscrits et des documents rares ou inédits.* (Paris: Alcan, 1901).

La Forge, Louis de. *Traité de l'âme humaine, de ses facultés et fonctions et de son union avec le corps, d'après les principes de Descartes.* (Paris: Girard, 1666.)

Rohault, Jacques. *Traité de physique.* (Paris: Savreux, 1671).

Régis, Pierre-Sylvain, *Système de philosophie, contenant la logique, la métaphysique, la physique et la morale.* (Lyon: Thierry, 1690).

Arnauld, Antoine. *Des Vrayes et des fausses idées, contre ce qu'ensigne l'auteur de la Recherche de la vérité.* (Cologne: Schouten, 1683).

[2] On Foucher see Chapter II.

Cartesianism (of which the second is his criticism of Malebranche of 1675, *Critique de la Recherche de la verité*)[1] give clearly the most important objections against Cartesian metaphysics. The system outlined below, while more complete than some and less complete than other expositions of Cartesian metaphysics, has the merit of including all those elements which played a role in the controversies which rocked Cartesianism. For us it will provide a background against which we can analyze the issues involved.

The late 17th century Cartesian system within which Foucher discovered problems can be characterized as follows: The universe consists of three substances, one uncreated and two created. God is an infinite substance Who creates mind and matter. Mind is unextended active *thinking*. Matter is unthinking passive *extension*. The two created substances differ in essence, and since it is their essences which *are* their characters as existents, they differ ontologically. There is no real difference between a substance and its essence. That is, mind is not a substance characterized by thinking; thinking *is* the substance of mind. This stresses the point that there is nothing in common between mind and matter; even though they are both substances created by God, they are entirely different as existents. This distinction between mind and matter is completely clear and distinct.

Matter is modified by the properties of size, shape, and motion or rest. These are the only properties a material thing can have. Mind is modified by will and intellect and by passions, volitions, sensations, and ideas. Ideas represent objects external to the mind; sensations do not. These are the only properties a mental thing can have. While substances exist in themselves either as uncreated or as created, modes exist only in created substances as their modifications. Everything is either a substance or a modification of a substance. This grouping of modifications of the two substances was thought in the 17th century to be Descartes' primary contribution to revolution in philosophy. Desgabets, for example, says that the insight which led to this distinction between material and mental properties shows that Descartes is the greatest philosopher since Aristotle.[2] The popular understanding of Scholastic philosophy as outlined by many Cartesians was that Scholastics believed that there were properties in material things similar to sensations.[3] Descartes rehearsed the traditional sceptical

---

[1] Foucher, Simon. *Critique de la Recherche de la verité où l'on examine en méme-tems une partie des Principes de Mr Descartes. Lettre, par un Academicien.* (Paris: Coustelier, 1675.)

[2] Lemaire, *op. cit.*, 39–42.

[3] *Ibid.*, 149.

arguments concerning the variation of sensations, illustrating the paradoxes which arise with the attribution of sensible properties to material things. It was considered a blow against both Scholasticism and scepticism to demonstrate that sensible properties *as* sensed are modifications not of a material, but of a mental substance.

Man is a union of mind and matter, the soul being the substantial form of the human body. Despite their essential difference, mind and matter interact. Ideas and sensations are caused through this interaction. In the case of ideas, whether they simply arise (having been innate) or are provided by God on the occasion of the interaction, or whether the action of matter on mind directly contributes to the content (and in this way causes the idea) is a point of contention. In either event, interaction is usually sufficient for and often necessary to the occurrence of ideas. Ideas of immaterial things can arise, of course, without interaction. Sometimes the will (with or without interaction) forms volitions which cause motions in matter; this is the reverse of the process by which motions in matter cause ideas. Passions also arise with or without interaction between mind and matter.

The mechanics of sensation and of perception are easily explained. The human body is so constructed that it has five kinds of sense organs which are connected to the brain by the nerves. When bodies of various kinds impinge upon these organs, motion is communicated from them through the nerves to the pineal gland which is the central organ in the brain. The motions caused in the pineal gland are uniformly distinctive dependent upon the various modifications of the material bodies and the sense-organs affected. Since space is extended, and extension is nothing more than matter, the material universe is a *plenum* in which subtle matter is everywhere; material bodies, therefore, do not always have to strike the sense organs themselves, but can act upon them through a medium in the manner that pulses of air put into motion by a vibrating body strike the ear drums. Hence, while the Cartesians disagree with Gassendi's assertion that a material species must travel from the material thing to the sense organ, they do agree that unmediated action cannot occur over a distance. And since distance is for the Cartesians nothing more than extension or matter, the very notion of action over an empty distance is inconceivable.

The pineal gland is the unifying organ of common sense and the seat of the soul. The occurrence of the distinctive motions in the pineal gland causes the mind to form sensations and ideas which are naturally and uniformly connected with these motions. And, certain volitions can cause (from the mind) other distinctive motions in the pineal gland which result in the movement of the human body. This far we can understand: there is a uniform causal interaction between the body and the soul. We can understand all the mechanics on the material side and can learn which ideas and sensations are naturally connected with which motions. We experience the interaction. But we cannot understand how the interaction takes place, *how* soul acts on body, or body on soul. It is a fact that God has arranged it so that interaction between body and soul takes place; we experience this interaction all the time; we can know no more.

The Cartesian way of ideas and the distinction between primary and secondary qualities is implicit in the sharp dualism of the created world. Ideas are representative modifications of the mind through which it knows things. There is no other way of knowing than by having ideas, for this is the nature of mind. Sensations are also modifications of the mind, but they are not representative; one does not have a sensation *of* a thing, though material things do cause sensations. Sensations serve only as signs by which man is advised as to whether his body should pursue or avoid material things in the interests of its own preservation. The Scholastics mistakenly attribute to material things sensible or secondary qualities similar to sensations. It is apparent that this is impossible when one considers that the modifications of mind are as utterly different from the modifications of matter as are the two substances from each other. There can be no kind of resemblance between the two modified substances: mind is active thinking; matter is inert extension.

A basic principle of Cartesian epistemology is that the knower must be directly acquainted with what is known. The mind is directly acquainted only with its own modifications. The Cartesians are committed to a representative theory of mediate knowledge because they can explicate the relation of direct acquaintance only in terms of the relation between a substance and its own modifications. Therefore, all knowledge of mental substance (that is, beyond direct intuitive knowledge of one's own mind), material substance, and the modifications of material substance is by way of ideas. These ideas are mental modifications whose nature it is to represent their objects. Descartes believed his own greatest contribution to philosophy was the discovery of the criterion for true ideas, that is, clearness and distinctness; many Cartesians took this as the rock upon which Cartesianism is built.

Finally, the Cartesians hold to the dictum that an idea must be caused by something which has as much or more formal or eminent reality as the idea has objective reality. This principle is meant to explain both how ideas can be caused, and how ideas can represent their objects. It derives from the basic axiom that something cannot come from nothing. This implies that there must be at least as much or more perfection in the cause as in the effect. Foucher took "'perfection" in this principle to mean "essential likeness" and thereby assumed that a basic principle of Cartesianism is that the cause must be like the effect to the extent that it is cause of the effect, or, conversely that the effect cannot be unlike the cause to the extent that it is effect of the cause. Besides this *causal likeness principle*, there is also a closely (but not necessarily) related epistemological principle which seems to be included in the Cartesian dictum that the objective reality of an idea cannot exceed the formal or eminent reality of its cause. The *epistemological likeness principle* is that the knower must in some essential way be like the known, or, conversely, that the known must in some essential way be like the knower. This seems to follow from the fact that an idea is essentially the mind modified, that is, a property of the mind. The mind is directly acquainted only with its own properties, and if these ideas must be in some way essentially like their objects in order to represent these objects, then the mind of which these ideas are properties must also be in some essential way like the mediately known objects. These two likeness principles are also important in Scholasticism, and were popularly expressed as like causes like, or like can only be caused by like, and as like knows like, or like can only be known by like. Foucher takes them for granted, and less obviously so does Malebranche. They form the basis for Foucher's objections to Cartesianism; he brings in the likeness principles to show that they cannot be satisfied in Cartesianism. He does this with the assumption that the Cartesians will want to retain these principles, and his assumption is justified (as is the inclusion of these principles in this model Cartesianism) by the fact that some of the Cartesians did attempt to show how the principles could be retained, while others gave them up only after a searching appraisal of what is important in Cartesian metaphysics as a whole.

The important principles of the model late 17th century Cartesiafnism sketched above, then, are as follows: (Note that this listing o-Cartesian principles is not meant to be complete; also, they are not necessarily phrased here in their most general form, but in a form most appropriate for the arguments which follow.) Ontologically, Cartesianism comprises:

(A)  God is an uncreated substance.
(B)  There is a dualism of two created substances which differ in essence: mind is *thinking*; matter is *extension*.
(C)  Volitions, passions, sensations, and ideas are the (only) modifications of mind.
(D)  Size, shape, and motion or rest are the (only) modifications of matter.
(E)  There is an all-inclusive ontological type-distinction between substance and modification; substance is dependent on nothing else (save God): modifications or properties are dependent upon substance.

There are three causal principles:

(F)  There is causal interaction between mind and matter.
(G)  Ideas and sensations are caused in some way by the interaction of matter and mind.
(H)  There must be essential likeness between a cause and its effect.

And five epistemological principles:

(I)  Ideas represent objects external to the mind.
(J)  Sensations do not represent objects external to the mind.
(K)  There must be essential likeness between an idea and its object.
(L)  Direct acquaintance is necessary for knowledge.
(M)  Objects external to the mind are known only by the mediate representation of ideas.

The arrival of Cartesians at such a system can be traced along many lines. The most obvious is that leading from methodic doubt in the *Mediations*. Beginning with the *cogito* and the simple bit of knowledge it provides, sheer lack of clutter allows the Cartesians, so they believe, to learn with certainty of the essences and properties of mind and matter. Another line leads from a set of self-evident (to Cartesians) principles of which the first is that nothing can have no properties. Volitions, passions, sensations, and ideas appear to Cartesians necessarily to be properties of one substance, while size, shape, and motion or rest seem necessarily to be properties of a different substance. They were also influenced by reasoning concerning mathematics and physics. Mathematical thinking can lead to belief in the permanence of quantitative properties at the expense of others in the conception of material things. And like Galileo, Cartesians do find that the real properties of material things are those which can be described in strict quantitative terms. Such a belief can either lead to or confirm the denial that qualitative properties really belong to material things. Cartesians find further evidence in experience, as does Gassendi, for suspecting the permanency of color, heat, and the other sensible qualities; their variations in the same thing are legion. Sceptics use such variations to show that knowledge of material things is uncertain. Cartesians, however, accuse sceptic and Scholastic alike of basing their arguments in childhood prejudice; it is a mistake to believe that the sensible qualities belong to material things. Such qualities are nothing more than sensations, modifications of the mind, whose variation is caused by changes in the real, quantitative properties of material things. Cartesians remove the whole field of error dependent upon sense limitations and illusions by making the distinction between primary and secondary qualities; the first are real properties of bodies of which we have ideas, the second are only sensations which are properties of the mind. The sceptics are right and the Scholastics deceived, for knowledge does not come by the senses, but by ideas. Sensations in themselves are what they are, and they lead to deception only if they are mistakenly judged to belong to or represent material things. With application one can learn which variations of the modifications of material things cause the different sensations. The purpose of sensations is to provide a quick, non-discursive set of natural signs designed by God toward the self-preservation of human bodies. Hence it is that lines of reasoning from psychological, metaphysical, logical, mathematical, physical, and sceptical considerations converge upon a system which implies the Cartesian way of ideas and the distinction between primary and secondary qualities.

Sufficient background has now been provided for our examination of the epistemological conflicts which led to the downfall of Cartesianism in the late 17th century. The Scholastic way of knowing involves a likeness between what is known (basically the form of the object) and the intelligible species through which or by which it is known. Whether this process is one of representation or of the sharing of essential form, the knowledge relationship rests upon the explanatory force of resemblance or similarity between the intelligible species and what is known. The Cartesian distinction between the essentially different substances, mind and matter, means that ideas which are modifications of the knowing mind can in no way be like the known material things. Cartesians, then, cannot utilize the explanatory force of resemblance to explain how ideas represent material things. As we shall see, they were forced to recognize this by being reminded of the ontological similarity between ideas and sensations. If sensations, because they are modifications of mind, cannot resemble supposed modifications of matter (secondary qualities) then neither can ideas which are also modifications of mind resemble actual modifications of matter (primary qualities). The Cartesians had to resolve the dilemma that neither or both ideas and sensations represent, for the distinction between ideas and sensations – and the closely related distinction between primary and secondary qualities – is one of the major foundations of Cartesianism, a foundation which distinguishes it from Scholasticism and opened the way to deductive mathematical physics.

We shall now state Foucher's objections to Cartesianism in summary form. Then, in Chapter IV, we shall examine in more detail his polemic with Malebranche in order to determine to what extent his criticisms apply also to Malebranchianism. The attempts of non-occasionalist Cartesians to seal the gaps in Cartesianism pointed out by Foucher will then be considered in Chapter V. Finally, in Chapter VI, the roots of Foucher's objections will be exposed and an analysis given of the failure of Malebranche and the Cartesians to meet Foucher's objections.

Foucher makes four basic criticisms of Cartesian metaphysics.[1] He first denies that causal interaction between mind and matter is possible on Cartesian principles. If mind and matter differ in essence, then there can be no possibility of any essential likeness or similarity between the two substances. Since some essential likeness is necessary for causal interaction between substances – so that they can engage one another, so to speak – it follows that no interaction is possible between mind and matter as defined by the Cartesians.

This leads Foucher to his second criticism: Cartesians evidently do not really know the essences of mind and matter. It seems obvious to Foucher that interaction does take place between mind and matter. It is further obvious to him that the causal likeness principle is self-evident. Consequently, the Cartesians must be wrong in their characterization of mind and matter as two substances differing in essence. The implication is that if they interact – as they do in fact – then they

---

[1] Foucher, Simon. *Critique de la Recherche de la verité où l'on examine en méme-tems une partie des Principes de Mr Descartes. Lettre, par un Academicien.* (Paris: Coustelier, 1675), 44ff.

must have some likeness in essence. Foucher points out that the Cartesians admit the interaction but deny the likeness, thus contradicting themselves.

The third criticism concerns the ontological similarity between sensations and ideas, both of which are said by the Cartesians to be modifications of the mind. Both, also, are caused by the interaction of material things with the mind. However, ideas are said to represent objects external to the mind, whereas sensations do not. But, Foucher insists, if ideas are mental modifications representative of material things which cause them, why do not sensations which are also modifications of the mind likewise represent the material things which cause them? In both cases it is the same material things which are the causes, and if the cause has anything to do with the representative nature of the effect – which to Foucher seems implied – then sensations as well as ideas surely could be representative. On the other hand, Foucher asks, if sensations do not represent material things, then how is it that ideas do? Nothing in the causal situation distinguishes ideas from sensations, and ontologically they are both modifications of mind. Hence, there is no reason for asserting that whatever is characteristic of the one is not also characteristic of the other. Foucher finds it obvious that ideas and sensations are similar in being modifications of the mind; he finds it arbitrary to distinguish ideas as representative from sensations which are not.

In this third criticism Foucher depends upon the link between the causal and the epistemological likeness principles which seems to be expressed in the Cartesian dictum that the cause of an idea must have at least as much or more formal or eminent reality as the idea has objective reality. He seems to have reasoned that ideas could represent the objects which cause them only on the ground that in causing an idea an object causes the idea to have an objective reality similar to the formal or eminent reality of the object. That is, there must be likeness between the object and the idea if there is to be a causal relationship. Now because of this likeness the object causes the idea, and also causes the idea to represent the object. So why is not the sensation which is also caused by the object likewise caused by the object to represent it? Finally, if an object cannot cause a sensation to represent it, then it must also be incapable of causing an idea to represent it.

The fourth criticism is deeper than the third, indeed, it goes to the heart of the matter. In Cartesian ontology mind and matter are substances which differ in essence. This difference Foucher takes to be ontological; it implies that there can be no similarity between mind and matter, nor any likeness between modifications of mind and modifications of matter. And if there is no resemblance, Foucher claims, there can be no representation. Ideas cannot *represent* material things or material modifications because ideas are mental modifications which can in no way *resemble* material things or material modifications.

Foucher here assumes that the required likeness between an idea and its object is ontological likeness. If mind and matter are essentially dissimilar, if *thinking* is completely different from *extension*, then no idea can be like matter. Foucher's criticism is to show that the Cartesian ontological dualism of created substances precludes adherence to the epistemological likeness principle. One cannot know material things by way of ideas on Cartesian principles.

Thus, just as the first two criticisms are based on an unqualified acceptance of the causal likeness principle, Foucher's fourth criticism is based on acceptance of the epistemological likeness principle. Foucher's four criticisms, with reference to the Cartesian principles outlined above, can be summarized as follows:

(*1*)  (F) cannot be true because of (B) which precludes the possibility of (H) upon which (F) depends.

(*2*)  (B) cannot be true because (F) and (H) are true, and (B) leads to (*1*).

(*3*)  (C) and (G) give no evidence for the distinction made in (I) and (J), but rather for the denial of this distinction.

(*4*)  Because of (B), (K) cannot be fulfilled, therefore (I) is impossible.

Foucher's criticisms were believed to be destructive of Cartesian metaphysics. The two criticisms concerning ideas in particular –(*3*)and (*4*) – were repeated by du Hamel, Bayle, and Huet.[1] Although Foucher's books were not widely read, Huet's were. And Bayle's *Dictionnaire* was a sourcebook for many philosophers including Locke, Berkeley, and Hume. Berkeley and Hume, for example, used Foucher's criticisms to dispute Locke's distinction between primary and secondary qualities.

---

[1] Du Hamel, Jean. *Réflexions critiques sur le système cartésienne de la philosophie de Mr. Régis.* (Paris: Couterot, 1692.)

Bayle, Pierre. *Dictionnaire historique et critique.* Cinquième edition, revue, corrigée, et augmentée. (Amsterdam: Brunel, 1740.) Tome III, Article "Pyrrhon" Remark B; Tome IV, Article "Zeno d'Elee", Remarks G and H.

Huet, Pierre-Daniel. *Censura Philosophiæ Cartesianæ.* (Paris: Horthemels, 1689.)

It seemed obvious that we do have knowledge of material things. Cartesian ontological dualism was thought to lead necessarily to an epistemology which is incapable of explaining – with reference to the likeness principles – how we have knowledge of material things. Hence, Cartesian metaphysics was denounced as false. Foucher traced the Cartesian difficulty ultimately to their dogmatic assertion that they know the essences of mind and matter. Obviously they do not, he claimed, for the metaphysical system built upon such assumed knowledge of the essences of these two substances leads to absurd conclusions.[1]

Therefore, to put it bluntly, Foucher insisted that something had to go. And as we shall see, all the solutions to Foucher's difficulties involve either denying the likeness principles or altering the ontological principles of Cartesianism.

There are at least five lines of development designed to meet problems raised in Cartesianism. These lines are through Malebranche, a number of orthodox (non-occasionalist) Cartesians, Locke, Spinoza, and Leibniz. The next three chapters contain characterizations and analyses of the solutions of Malebranche and the orthodox Cartesians to Cartesian problems. We thus see what these philosophers thought was essential in Cartesianism. Then a brief consideration will be given to the question of whether Foucher's criticisms apply to Descartes' philosophy as contrasted to Cartesianism. It will be seen that the difficulties detected by Foucher are inherent in the foundations of Cartesianism.

With this perspective, we can view in Chapter VII the post-Cartesian development of the Cartesian way of ideas through Locke, Berkeley, and Hume. Locke can be seen as still struggling to repair Cartesian metaphysics, but his repairs contribute as much to its final debacle as do the positive criticisms – drawn upon a Foucherian model – of Berkeley and Hume.

The possible solutions of Spinoza and Leibniz are but briefly mentioned since they are outside the direct line of this study. However, because of Lebniz's important relations with Foucher, his solution is treated at more length in Chapter VIII.

---

[1] Foucher, Simon. *Dissertations sur la recherche de la verité, contenant l'histoire et les principes de la philosophie des academiciens, avec plusieurs réflexions sur les sentimens de M. Descartes.* (Paris: Anisson, 1693), 187–188.

# THE CONTROVERSY CONCERNING IDEAS BETWEEN MALEBRANCHE AND FOUCHER

The first volume of the first edition of *De la recherche de la verité où l'on traite de la nature de l'esprit de l'homme, et de l'usage qu'il en doit faire pour éviter l'erreur des sciences* by Nicolas Malebranche appeared in 1674.[1] No volume number is given and the only indication that the three books it contains do not constitute a complete work is a one-sentence paragraph in Chapter IV of Book I which lists six topics to be treated; the volume closes with the word FIN. It is not surprising, then, to find Simon Foucher publishing his short *Critique de la Recherche de la verité où l'on examine en méme-tems une partie des Principes de Mr Descartes* in 1675 [2] under the impression that he was examining a completed work. He was soon apprised of his oversight; Malebranche responded in the preface to the second volume with one of the nastiest printed attacks in the history of philosophy (Descartes' opinion of Pere Bourdin is comparable, but was not meant for the public) which is crowned with the now famous line: "Quand on Critique un Livre, il me semble qu'il faut au moins l'avoir lû." [3]

The following short exposition of the theory of ideas found in this first volume is developed from the assumption that Foucher did read it. Several expositions of Malebranche's theory of ideas have been given, but they have all been based on the complete edition of the *Recherche* which contains numerous revisions and clarifications, some of which are meant to counter Foucher's objections or to keep readers from making the misunderstandings Foucher supposedly makes. The

[1] Malebranche, Nicolas. *Oeuvres complètes.* 20 volumes. Direction: André Robinet (Paris: J. Vrin, 1958–). The first volume of the first edition of 1674 is available in volume I of this edition: it is referred to hereafter as *Recherche* and all references are to it.

[2] Foucher, Simon. *Critique de la Recherche de la verité où l'on examine en méme-tems une partie des Principes de Mr Descartes. Lettre, par un Academicien* (Paris: Martin Coustelier, 1675). Hereafter referred to as *Critique.*

[3] Malebranche. *op. cit.,* II, Préface Pour servir de Réponse à la critique du premier Volume, 496.

exposition in this chapter, however, is based on how Foucher must have read the first volume of the first edition. From his objections in the *Critique* and his responses to Malebranche's reply, it is evident that Foucher detects two theories of ideas in the first volume of the *Recherche*, the second of which he takes to be a spurious expression of piety not suited to philosophical discussion. Foucher's important argument concerning primary and secondary qualities is made against the theory he finds most strongly developed, a Cartesian theory which Malebranche disowns in the preface to the second volume. It can be contended that the first volume of the *Recherche* shows the development of the Malebranchian theory of ideas seen in God from the orthodox Cartesian view; this is implicitly argued for in the following. Here it is shown that Foucher must have interpreted the *Recherche* in this way. He finds the Cartesian view treated most thoroughly in the first volume and has good reason for believing that it is Malebranche's. He is shocked when Malebranche announces that the Cartesian theory is not his own, and can see the vision in God only as a grasping at theological straws by one who has grappled unsuccessfully with the problems of the Cartesian way. Hence, as we shall see, in his *Réponse pour la Critique à la Preface du second volume de la Recherche de la verité, où l'on examine le sentiment de M. Descartes touchant les idées* of 1676,[1] Foucher merely stresses one aspect of his argument to meet Malebranche's parry; he does not alter it. Nor do Malebranche's revisions and clarifications cause Foucher to alter his argument in later critiques. Foucher believes that the theory of the vision in God makes ideas as difficult to know as are material things.

In the first volume of the first edition of the *Recherche* Malebranche points out that the human soul has two major faculties, understanding and will. We shall confine our exposition to the understanding. The understanding is "la capacité de recevoir differentes idées et différentes modifications dans l'esprit." It "est entierement passive et ne renferme aucune action."

D'où il faut conclure que c'est l'entendement seul qui aperçoit, puisqu'il n'y a que lui qui reçoive les idées des objets; car c'est une même chose à l'âme d'apercevoir un objet ou de recevoir l'idée qui le represente. C'est aussi l'entendement qui aperçoit les modifications de l'ame, puisque j'entends, par ce mot *entendement* cette faculté passive de l'ame par laquelle elle

---

[1] Foucher, Simon. *Réponse pour la Critique à la Preface du second volume de la Recherche de la verité, ou l'on examine le sentiment de M. Descartes touchant les idées, avec plusieurs remarques utiles pour les sciences* (Paris: Charles Angot, 1676). Hereafter referred to as *Réponse pour la Critique à la Preface*.

reçoit toutes les differentes modifications dont elle est capable; & que c'est la même chose à l'âme de recevoir la maniere d'être qu'on appelle la douleur, que d'apercevoir la douleur; puisqu'elle ne peut recevoir la douleur d'autre maniere qu'en l'apercevant.

From this it can be concluded that "c'est l'entendement qui imagine les objets absens, & qui sent ceux qui sont presens; & que le *sens* & *l'imagination* ne sent que l'entendement, appercevant les objets par les organes du corps." [1] Since the understanding is passive, that is, it does not originate its perceptions but is only the capacity for them to occur in the mind, it is obvious that it does not judge in perception. Besides knowing, sensing, and imagining, the understanding also remembers and has passions.

Idea is both a general and a specific term for Malebranche:

les idées de l'ame sont de deux sortes en prenant le nom d'idée en général, pour tout ce que l'esprit aperçoit immediatement. Les premieres nous representent quelque chose hors de nous, comme celle d'un quarré, d'un triangle, etc. & les secondes ne nous representent que ce qui se passe dans nous comme nos sensations, la douleur, le plaisir, etc. Car on fera voir dans la suite que ces dernieres idées ne sont rien autre chose qu'une maniere d'estre de l'esprit; & c'est pour cela que je les appellerai de *modifications* de l'esprit. [2]

These second ideas, which are non-representative and nothing more than modifications of the spirit, are usually called sensations. The first sort of ideas, those which represent external objects, are usually referred to simply as ideas or "pures perceptions." In simple perception these ideas are of simple things; in connection with judgments, the ideas the understanding knows are of relations among things; and in reasoning what is known are ideas of relations among relations.

There are four things which might be confused in having a sensation: (1) The action of the material thing. (2) The passion of the sense organs which are agitated, this agitation being communicated along the nerves to the brain. (3) The passion of the soul which is the sensation properly speaking. (4) A judgment that what is sensed is in the sense organ and in the material thing. The mistaken notion that there are sensible qualities in material things arises because this judgment is so prompt and habitual it is taken for a simple sensation. There is no causal relation between sensations (3) and the motions (1) and (2) of material things (including the sense organs and the brain) except that God has willed that they are reciprocal. This means that there

---

[1] *Recherche, I,* 43.
[2] *Ibid.,* 42.

need not necessarily (except for God's willing it) be a material thing present for one to have a sensation. However, material things are the only things perceivable in sensation, for they are the only things capable of making impressions upon the sense organs.

C'est ainsi qu'elle voit des plaines & des rochers présens à ses yeux, qu'elle connaît la dureté du fer, & la pointe d'une épée & choses semblables; & ces sortes de perceptions s'appellent *sentimens*.[1]

Our senses never deceive us. "Quand on voit, par exemple, de la lumiére, il est très-certain que l'on voit de la lumiére." Error arises when we judge that what we sense is outside the soul. One must follow this rule:

*De ne juger jamais par les sens de la verité absolue des choses; ni de ce qu'elles sont en elles-mêmes, mais seulement du rapport qu'elles ont avec nôtre corps,* parce qu'en effet ils ne nous sont point donnez pour connoître la vérité des choses en elles-mêmes, mais seulement pour la conservation de nôtre corps.[2]

Light, color, heat, cold pleasure, and pain are definitely modifications of the soul. As for other sensations of material things:

nos yeux nos trompent generalement en tout ce qu'ils nous représentent, dans la grandeur des corps, dans leur figure & dans leurs mouvemens, dans la lumiére & dans les couleurs, qui sont les seules choses que nous voyons ... toutes ces choses ne sont point telles qu'elles nous paroissent.[3]

The things we see and the distinctions of size, figure, and movement that we can make by our senses are proportional to the size of our bodies. Reason tells us that there are worlds within worlds upon fleas. We cannot comprehend such a manifold extension in all its infinity, let alone perceive it in sensation.

Nôtre vûë ne nous représente donc point l'étenduë selon qu'elle est en elle-même, mais seulement ce qu'elle est par rapport à nôtre corps; & parce que la moitié d'un mite n'a pas un rapport considérable à nôtre corps, & que cela ne peut ni le conserver ni le détruire, nôtre vûë nous le cache entiére-ment.[4]

Not only is visible extension proportional to our bodies, because of the differences of men's eyes every man sees a different extension, one which is proportional to his body alone. This is quite adequate, for "l'exactitude & la justesse ne sont point essentielles aux connaissances sensibles, qui ne doivent servir qu'à la conservation de la vie."[5]

[1] *Ibid.*, 67.
[2] *Ibid.*, 77–78.
[3] *Ibid.*, 79.
[4] *Ibid.*, 84.
[5] *Ibid.*, 92.

Although we cannot know by sensations the absolute size, figure, or motion of any material thing, we can know the relations among things. We can even know of the relations among the infinite number of extensions that are sensed; that is, we can reason that there are probably parasites on fleas which seem about the same size to the fleas as do fleas to us.

Il est donc constant que les jugements que nous faisons touchant l'étenduë, les figures, & les mouvemens des corps, renferment donc quelque vérité: mais il n'en est pas de même de ceux que nous faisons touchant la lumiére, couleurs, & toutes les autres qualitez sensibles; car la vérité ne s'y recontre jamais.[1]

Hence, when we are precipitated into the judgment in sensation that a falling rock has the size, figure, and motion we see, our judgment is not completely incorrect. We do know its size, figure, and motion relative to the size, figure, and motion of our own body. And though these things as seen are inaccurate so far as knowledge of the absolute size, figure, and motion of these bodies with relation to true extension is concerned, there is a relationship between what we see and the absolute properties; the proportions still hold. However, our judgments that material things are of a certain color, or have any of the other sensible qualities, are completely wrong. There is no corresponding set of colors, odors, etc. belonging to material things as there is a world of real extension corresponding to the extension we see.

As the sensation is the faculty for perceiving material things when they are present to cause an image in the brain, the imagination is the soul's faculty for perceiving material things when they are absent;

elle se les représente en s'en formant des images dans le cerveau. C'est de cette maniére qu'on imagine toutes sortes de figures, un cercle, un triangle, un visage, un cheval, des villes & des campagnes, soit qu'on les ait déjà vûës ou non. Ces sortes de perceptions s'appellent *imaginations*, parce que l'ame se représente ces objets en s'en formant des images dans le cerveau.

It follows that one cannot imagine spiritual things "parce qu'on ne peut pas se former des images des choses spirituelles." [2]

The third faculty of the soul is the pure understanding.

Elle aperçoit par *l'entendement pur* les choses spirituelles, les universelles, les notions communes, l'idée de la perfection, celle d'un être infiniment parfait, & toutes ses pensées, comme ses inclinations naturelles, ses passions & ses perceptions. Elle aperçoit même par l'entendement pur les choses

[1] *Ibid.*, 122.
[2] *Ibid.*, 66.

matérielles, l'étenduë avec ses propriétez; car il n'y a que l'entendement pur qui puisse apercevoir un cercle, & un quarré parfait, une figure de mille côtez, & choses semblables. Ces sortes de perceptions s'appellent *pures intellections*, ou *pures perceptions*, parce que l'esprit ne se forme point d'images corporelles dans le cerveau pour se représenter toutes ces choses.[1]

The pure understanding, then, is "la faculté qu'a l'esprit de connaître les objets de dehors, sans en former d'images corporelles dans le cerveau." [2]

The soul perceives two sorts of things, one kind in the soul and the other kind outside the soul:

Celles qui sont dans l'ame sont ses propres pensées, c'est-à-dire toutes ses diffé-rentes modifications, car par ces mots, *pensée, maniére de penser*, ou *modification de l'âme*, j'entends généralement toutes les choses, qui ne peuvent être dans l'ame sans qu'elle les aperçoive: comme sont ses propres sensations, ses imaginations, ses pures intellections, ou simplement ses conceptions, ses passions mêmes, & ses inclinations naturelles ... que l'ame mesme d'une telle, ou telle façon ... elle n'a pas besoin d'idée pour les apercevoir.[3]

In summary, one does not need an idea to perceive an idea. Things outside the soul can be perceived only by means of ideas; these things are either material or spiritual. Malebranche is certain that no one will dispute that we know them by way of ideas:

Je crois que tout le monde tombe d'accord que nous n'appercevons point les choses qui sont hors de nous par elles-mesmes, mais seulement par les idées que nous en avons. ... l'objet immédiat de nôtre esprit, lorsqu'il voit le Soleil, n'est pas le Soleil, mais quelque chose qui est intimement unie à nôtre ame; & c'est ce que j'appele *idée*. Ainsi par ce mot *idée*, je n'entends ici autre chose que ce qui est l'objet immédiat, ou le plus proche de l'esprit, quand il aperçoit quelque chose.[4]

Although an idea is necessary if an external thing is to be perceived, it is not necessary for anything external to be present for one to have an idea.

When we conceive the idea of a square, for example, we can at the same time imagine it, "c'est-à-dire l'apercevoir en nous en traçant une image dans le cerveau."

L'image d'un quarré par example, que l'imagination trace dans le cerveau, n'est juste & bien fait que par la conformité qu'elle a avec l'idée d'un quarré que nous concevons par la pure intellection. C'est cette idée qui

---

[1] *Ibid.*
[2] *Ibid.*, 381.
[3] *Ibid.*, 415.
[4] *Ibid.*, 413–414.

regle cette image. C'est l'esprit qui conduit l'imagination, & qui l'oblige de regarder de tems en tems, si l'image qu'elle peint est une figure de quatre lignes droites & égales, dont les angles soient exactement droits: en un mot si ce qu'on image est semblable à ce qu'on conçoit.[1]

In reading this passage, Foucher must have taken it to mean that the idea is similar to the material image in the brain. That is, he takes "regle" in the above passage in the sense of to regulate by being a physical model. He might then wonder if Malebranche means that the idea is like the material image which in turn is like the material thing. He would certainly detect some confusion here. A few pages later Malebranche says that "l'image que le Soleil imprime dans le cerveau ne ressemble point à l'idée que l'ame en a."[2] If Foucher interprets the the previous passage as we have suggested, he cannot help but find a contradiction here. Malebranche adds that "toutes les sensations & toutes les passions de l'ame ne representent rien hors d'elle, qui leur ressemble, & que ce ne sont que des modifications dont un esprit est capable." [3]

Foucher must have found this extremely confusing, or more probably, he took it as an indication that Malebranche was confused. The many Cartesian elements in the work led Foucher to interpret Malebranche's theory of ideas as Cartesian. Malebranche speaks of pure intellections and conceptions as modifications of the soul, and he speaks of the idea of a square as something conceived in the mind. Ideas are most intimately united to our souls. Hence, ideas, like sensations, cannot resemble material things for they are modifications of an immaterial substance. This is the source of Foucher's first major objection. Why should ideas be singled out as representative when sensations are not? He finds his second objection in Malebranche's (on Foucher's interpretation) confusion. Malebranche says that ideas resemble material images in the brain which in turn resemble material things. How, Foucher asks, is this possible? How can an idea be a model for a material image traced by imagination in the brain? How can we know a material thing by an idea which cannot resemble it? Even if it were suggested that in the passages quoted above "regle" should be interpreted as "directions for the construction of," Foucher would no doubt say that the problem of comparing what is conceived in the instructions with the product still remains.

[1] *Ibid.*, 425–426.
[2] *Ibid.*, 431.
[3] *Ibid.*, 433.

What can be done with such a mix-up? Foucher sees Malebranche doing the only reasonable thing. Malebranche drops it and begins a new chapter.

In discussing sensations and imaginations, Malebranche had said that they are nothing more than modifications of the soul, meaning, as Foucher reads it, that they are non-representative. Then follows a passage which Foucher must have seen as anomalous, for it contradicts the presentation of pure ideas as modifications of the soul:

les idées simples des objets de la pure intellection ... bien que présentes à l'esprit ne le touchent ni ne le modifient pas. ... toutes les idées abstraites ne modifient point l'ame ... toutes les sensations la modifient.[1]

This is the only passage Foucher needs to discount to read Malebranche as a Cartesian in his way of ideas. And, as we have seen, there are later passages which seem to make it clear that ideas are intimately united with the soul (and hence touch it) and also are modifications of it.

Now, however, Malebranche follows up this anomalous passage. We see all things in God. God is the place of ideas; "il est absolument nécessaire que Dieu ait en lui-même idées de toutes les choses, qu'il a créees, puisqu'autrement il n'auroit pas pû les produire." [2] Is this because they are necessary as models? Are they modifications of God? This is not clear. What is clear is that we have a new theory in which ideas are not modifications of man's soul, which, to Foucher, seems based on nothing more than a pious phrase conjured up to screen the debacle of the Cartesian way of ideas. When we perceive a material thing, God causes us to have a sensation (He does not have them Himself) and at the same time:

Pour l'idée qui se trouve jointe avec le sentiment, elle est en Dieu, & nous la voyons parce qu'il lui plaît de nous la découvrir : & Dieu joint la sensation à l'idée alors que les objets sont présens, afin que nous le croyions ainsi, & que nous entrions dans les sentiments, où nous devons estre par rapport à eux.[3]

God is the intelligible world and in Him is the general idea of extension which "suffit pour faire connaître toutes les proprietez, dont l'étendüe est capable." [4] This idea of extension is perhaps also the idea of infinity, for "toutes ces idés particuliéres [celles de l'esprit] ne sont

---

[1] *Ibid.*, 408.
[2] *Ibid.*, 437.
[3] *Ibid.*, 445.
[4] *Ibid.*, 450.

que des participations de l'idée générale de l'infini." And perhaps it is also the idea of God; "il n'est pas possible que Dieu ait d'autre fin principale de ses actions que lui même." [1]

> Dieu ne peut donc faire un esprit pour connoître ses ouvrages, si ce n'est que cet esprit voie en quelque façon Dieu en voyant ses ouvrages. . . . nous ne voyons aucune chose que par la connaissance naturelle que nous avons de Dieu. Toutes les idées particuliéres que nous avons des créatures, ne sont que des determinations generales de l'idée du Créateur.[2]

The particular ideas we have of material things, then, are particularizations or limitations of the idea of extension, of the idea of infinity, and of the idea of God. The first is in God and may or may not be the same as the second; the third also must be in God and may or may not be the same as the second.

Foucher, then, sees two theories of ideas in the first volume of the first edition of the *Recherche*. The first is Cartesian: pure ideas and sensations are modifications of the soul, modifications which cannot resemble material things; however, the ideas are said to represent material things, and to resemble material images in the brain. Malebranche could not extract himself from this tangle, so Foucher believes, hence the second theory of ideas is offered: ideas are not modifications of the soul; they are in God who allows us to see them when appropriate; through them we know material things. No further explanation is given of how they are in God nor of the relation they have to our souls when we know them. Foucher certainly saw the need for a different theory of ideas than the Cartesian one, but he took the notion of seeing ideas in God as nothing more on Malebranche's part than a pious afterthought. As we have seen, Foucher, or any other contemporary, needed little more than the expectation that he would find the Cartesian theory of ideas in Malebranche to allow him to discover it as the one Malebranche held to be philosophically (as opposed to theologically) important. Malebranche later developed the vision in God theory to some extent, but as Foucher himself (and later Arnauld) pointed out, it is less explanatory than the defective Cartesian theory and subject to the same or even graver difficulties.

We see here in Foucher's eyes, if not in fact, the development of Malebranche's major deviation from Descartes – his theory of ideas. In this first expression are seen quite plainly the traces of its Cartesian origin. In grasping these traces Foucher presents his threat to the

---

[1] *Ibid.*, 441–442.
[2] *Ibid.*, 252.

Cartesian way of ideas. And when he later allows that Malebranche is making a major effort to break away from the Cartesian theory and thus avoid the troubles to which it is subject, Foucher never forgets the new theory's parenthood and claims that the offspring is heir to a tendency to suffer from the sire's ailments.

In 1673 Foucher had a small number of copies of his *Dissertations sur la recherche de la verité, ou sur la logique des academiciens* printed in Dijon.[1] In it he speaks of the need for workers in "la recherche de la verité." This perhaps gave him some grounds for believing that Malebranche's Recherche of 1674 was in response to the call in the *Logique* of 1673, though Malebranche's title is not an uncommon one. Whether or not he seriously believed that Malebranche was inspired by the *Logique*, Foucher states that the *Critique de la Recherche*, like the prior *Logique* and the *Recherche*, is conceived as an aid in the search for truth. By pointing out some of the errors made by Descartes and Malebranche he feels he can further the cause for certainty. The principles he uses in doing so are such as no man of good sense will deny; they are the laws of the Academic philosophers which are as follows:

(1) *Ne se conduire que par Demonstration en matiere de Philosophie.*
(2) *Ne point agiter les questions que nous voions bien ne pouvoir decider.*
(3) *Avoüer que l'on ne sçait pas, ce que l'on ignore effectivement.*
(4) *Distinguer les choses que l'on sçait de celles que l'on ne sçait pas.*
(5) *Chercher toûjours des connoissances nouvelles.*[2]

Foucher points out that in the search for knowledge, first principles should be inquired into because they are necessary for founding true demonstrations.[3] This is the only way of avoiding error in judgment. Malebranche, however, who says he is going to show how to avoid error, does not do this.[4] Malebranche violates the first rule in the search for truth; he assumes that he has already found it. His system is based on fourteen assumptions, all of which can be challenged. Foucher treats them in turn. The first seven assumptions are, in somewhat abbreviated form, as follows:

---

[1] Foucher, Simon. *Dissertations sur la recherche de la verité, ou sur la logique des academiciens* (Dijon: publisher unknown, 1673). Hereafter referred to as *Logique.*
[2] Foucher, Simon. *Dissertation sur la recherche de la verité, contenant l'apologie des academiciens, où l'on fait voir que leur maniere de philosopher est la plus utile pour la religion, & la plus conforme au bon sens, pour servir de Réponse à la Critique de la Critique, &c. avec plusieurs remarques sur les erreurs des sens & sur l'origine de la philosophie de Monsieur Descartes* (Paris: Estienne Michallet, 1687), 5–8, 44–45. (Hereafter referred to as *Apologie.*)
[3] *Critique*, 4.
[4] *Ibid.*, 13.

(1) That the soul of man is a simple indivisible substance without parts which is neither material nor extended.
(2) That there are two kinds of truth: necessary and contingent.
(3) That the mysteries of faith can be appealed to in philosophy.
(4) That pure intellection is not accompanied by brain traces.
(5) That we have two kinds of ideas: those (ideas) which represent what is outside us and those (sensations) which represent only what is within us.
(6) That our ideas need not resemble the objects they represent.
(7) That extension, figures, and motions have real existence independent of our mind.[1]

Foucher's major objections to what he believes is Malebranche's theory of ideas are contained in his remarks on assumptions (5), (6), and (7).

Assumption (5) states that we have two kinds of ideas: those (ideas) which represent what is outside us and those (sensations) which represent what is within us. Foucher says that Malebranche recognizes that both kinds are immediately and truly known. It would seem, then, difficult to distinguish ideas from sensations since they appear to us equally as modifications of the soul. Both or neither of them must represent external things. Further, since according to Malebranche the soul has nothing in it similar to matter or extension, Foucher cannot see how it can represent anything except its own unextended ideas.[2] He says that "ces Idées ... ne nous representent que les effets, que les Objets exterieurs produisent en Nous & non pas ce qu'ils sont en eux-méme." [3] He believes that Malebranche recognizes this difficulty and perhaps has offered the vision in God to remedy it. But the only argument Malebranche offers for establishing his new theory is that all other hypotheses of how we know external things are false, so the theory of the vision in God is true. Foucher says this is not a good argument.[4] The notion of seeing all things in God is true in a broad, theological sense, of course, and is a fine and pious sentiment. But, Foucher points out in his remarks on assumption (3), such theological remarks have no place in serious philosophical discussions and should be reserved for sermons.[5]

Assumption (6) states that our ideas need not resemble the objects

---

[1] *Ibid.*, 21, 25, 32, 36, 44, 50, 62.
[2] *Ibid.*, 44–45.
[3] *Ibid.*, 47.
[4] *Ibid.*, 48–49.
[5] *Ibid.*, 32–33.

they represent. If this is true, Foucher first says, then there are no
grounds for asserting that our sensations are completely unlike what
causes them; they, too, might be representative, for if resemblance
is not required, any idea or sensation could represent. What is more,
they might all represent the same object. Foucher claims that Malebranche takes this view from Descartes who may not have meditated
on it too much because he needs it to preserve the notion of matter
which is essential to his physics.[1] But, above all, Foucher finds that
non-resembling representative ideas are incomprehensible:

On n'entend autre chose par *representer*, si-non rendre une chose presente,
ou faire le méme effet qui si elle agissoit actuellement, ou du-moins en faire
un *semblable*, autrement on ne sçait ce qu'on veut dire par ce mot.[2]

Even if ideas have effects on our souls similar to those material things
have, the ideas still cannot represent these material things for we do
not know what the things are in themselves and so cannot compare
them with ideas; besides, Malebranche admits that the effects are not
similar to the things that cause them. Foucher points out that Malebranche at least does not fall into the error of thinking that we can know
external things by images in the brain. Our ideas no more resemble
these material images than they do the external things.[3]

As for the Cartesian appeal to the fact that "arbre" represents a
tree without resembling it, Foucher says this argument rests on a
double equivocation. In the first place, it is not the word which is
supposed to be representative in this case, but the idea to which the
word gives rise. And in the second place, the idea itself is not representative of the tree, but only of the effect the tree causes in our soul.
The word cannot represent the tree in itself, for we have no idea of the
tree in itself. The only way that words can be said to represent things
is that we can be trained to have the same ideas upon the occurrence of
words as we would upon the presence of things. If we could know
exterior things in themselves, we might find that our ideas are no more
similar to them than words are to ideas. This is the final absurdity in
suggesting that ideas can be representative of things they do not
resemble. Foucher closes his discussion by stating that everyone is well-
assured that we cannot know things in themselves. It necessarily
follows either that our ideas do not represent them or that our ideas

---

[1] *Ibid.*, 50–52.
[2] *Ibid.*, 52.
[3] *Ibid.*, 53–56.

resemble things in themselves; since the latter is impossible, the former must be true.[1]

Assumption (7) is that extension, figures, and motions that we see have real existence outside our minds. Foucher complains that Malebranche fails to prove that the judgments we make about these properties have more truth than judgments we make about light, color, and the other sensible qualities. Descartes assumes the same thing. Foucher says Cartesians base this assumption on the fact that we have ideas of thinking and extension, two things which seem to have nothing in common. Since thinking seems to be what the soul is, they take extension to be matter. Foucher says it can be doubted 1) that our ideas of thinking do not contain something of extension, 2) that the same subject cannot support both thinking and extension, at least at different times, and 3) that some of our ideas are not modifications of our soul to which there is nothing similar outside us.[2]

Foucher recalls a discussion he had on knowledge of external material things with Rohault in 1667. Rohault supported Descartes' opinion that sensations are mere passions produced in our soul similar to nothing in material objects. Foucher asked that if this is the case, then why is it not concluded that the extension known by the senses is also nothing more than a "Façon-d'estre de Nostre Ame" similar to nothing in material things? Rohault's reply was that we do not know extension by the senses. Foucher was very surprised at this answer, for it is evident that we know light and color by the senses; when one sees a red square, for example, one sees at the same time its color, figure, and extension. It is even the case that extension is known by two senses, those of sight and touch. Even Malebranche, Foucher insists, agrees that we know (sensible) extension by the senses. For Foucher, it is as obvious that we know extension by the senses as that there is light at noon. However, he restrained his surprise long enough to ask Rohault how we do know extension, if not by the senses. Rohault replied that we know extension by reason. We observe, for example, that objects touch us at different points, so conclude that they are extended. Foucher points out that this either means that the soul is extended – which has been denied – or it begs the question; unless we know already that different sensations are caused from different places, we cannot conclude from having them that their causes are extended.[3]

---

[1] *Ibid.*, 56–60.
[2] *Ibid.*, 61–64.
[3] *Ibid.*, 64–66, 77–78. (The pagination jumps from 66 to 77; because of this mistake there are no pages 67–76.)

One just cannot distinguish ideas from sensations:

> Car toutes nos Sensations n'estant autres Choses que des Experiences de plusieurs Façons-d'Estre dont Nostre Ame est capable. Nous ne connoissons veritablement par les Sens que Ce que les Objects produisent en Nous, d'où il s'ensuit qui si on avoüe que Nous connoissons de l'Estendüe & des Figures par le Sens aussi bien que de la Lumiere & des Couleurs, il faudra conclure necessairement que cette Estendüe & ces Figures ne sont pas moins en Nous que cette Lumiere & ces Couleurs.
>
> Et quand on voudroit accorder ce Privilege à l'Estendüe qu'elle seroit dans Nostre Ame & dans les Objets exterieurs, au-lieu que les Couleurs ne seroient que dans Nostre Ame: ce seroit tousiours avoüir que la perception que Nous en aurions par les Sens Nous la seroit reconnoister pour une Façon-d'Estre de Nostre Ame, ce qui d'estruiroit encore le Systéme de Monsieur DESCARTES, outre que de soustenir que l'Ame & la Matiere sont capables d'une méme Façon-d'estre, ce seroit avanser une chose encore plus opposée aux Principes de ce Philosophe que celle que l'on voudroit éviter par cette Réponse.[1]

In summary, Foucher objects to Malebranche that ideas cannot be distinguished as representative from sensations which are not, for they are both modifications of the soul; both or neither must be representative. And since the soul is spiritual, none of its modifications can represent material things which are extended: neither sensations nor ideas – which are unextended – can resemble them. The criticisms are of the Cartesian way of ideas, which, for good reasons, Foucher believes Malebranche to hold. He criticizes the vision in God here only by denying assumption (3) that the mysteries of faith can be appealed to in philosophy. He has expressed, however, the criticism he later stresses against the vision in God: if represent does not mean resemblance, it is unintelligible.

Foucher did not have to wait long for Malebranche's reply.

Malebranche's response to Foucher's *Critique* appears in the second volume of the *Recherche* in 1675 as "Preface Pour servir de Réponse à la critique de premier Volume." [2] Malebranche is most incensed about Foucher's assumption that the first volume contains a method: he quotes the sentence outlining the parts of the work and points out that only the first three parts are included in the first volume. As for the assumptions Foucher accuses him of holding, Malebranche says that they are all incidental propositions, propositions drawn from examples, or responses to objections. Foucher attributes these opinions to him out of failure to comprehend the text. After making it abundantly

---

[1] *Ibid.*, 79–80.
[2] Malebranche, *op cit.*, 480–499.

clear that he does not believe that it is worthwhile, Malebranche answers Foucher's objections about what is called his first assumption, and then prints what Foucher has to say about the second and third in columns side by side with his own replies. He says he would continue through the whole *Critique* in such fashion if he thought anyone was interested. However, it can easily be seen that Foucher "n'a presque jamais pris mon sens & qu'il n'a aucune idée de mon dessein": [1] because of this Malebranche does not believe that any reasonable person would be interested. Hence, he closes with a few words concerning the rest of the assumptions Foucher accuses him of making. He believes that his thorough refutation of Foucher's first three criticisms shows "ce qu'on doit penser des autres auxquels je n'ai répondu qu'en deux mots." [2] Since it is our contention that Foucher does offer important objections to Malebranche's way of ideas, we shall examine carefully the few words Malebranche does have in response concerning the fifth, sixth, and seventh assumptions. It is worth seeing why he does not think an answer is necessary. Malebranche says of Foucher concerning the fifth assumption:

> Il m'impose dans son cinquième Chapitre plusieurs sentimens, que je n'ai pas. Il n'est point vrai que *je reconnaisse que toutes nos idées ne sont que des façons d'être de nôtre ame.* J'ay fait au contraire dans le troisiéme Livre qu'il critique, un chapitre exprés pour prouver que cette opinion est insoûtenable. Quand on Critique un Livre, il me semble qu'il faut au moins l'avoir lû. Il n'est point encore vrai, *que je reconnaisse, que les idées que nous recevons par les sens, ne nous représentent que les effets que les objets extérieurs produisent en nous:* j'ai dit le contraire en plusieurs endroits, dans le Chapitre quinziéme du premier Livre & ailleurs. [3]

Malebranche evidently had not read Foucher's *Critique* with too much care, for in Chapter XV of Book I Malebranche discusses the changes which take place in the retinal nerves during the perception of light[4]; it is not these effects that Foucher is talking about, but the sensations themselves as we experience them. As for the "chapitre exprés," Malebranche must be referring to Chapter VI of Book III. "*Que nous voyons toutes choses en Dieu.*" Here he says that in the perception of a sensible thing there are two elements: "*sentiment* et *idée* pure. Le sentiment est une modification de nôtre ame." But "l'idée qui se trouve

---

[1] *Ibid.*, 459–496.
[2] *Ibid.*, 498.
[3] *Ibid.*, 496.
[4] *Ibid.*, I, 162–164.

jointe avec le sentiment, elle est en Dieu."[1] Foucher comments in the *Critique* on this chapter by praising Malebranche's piety, but insists that such a remark could hardly be a philosophical principle. He goes on to say that even if ideas were in God, this still does not solve the problem of how we can know material things. God is, if anything, more immaterial than our own souls. One is still faced with all the problems of non-resembling representative ideas.[2] Even more, Malebranche's pious remark could not be taken seriously for the following reason:

> Il faut qu'il resulte quelque Façon-d'Estre dans nostre Ame, pour qüe nous ayons de la Connoissance: parce que la Connoissance, comme on a coûtume de le dire, est une Action *immanente*, ou si l'on veut c'est une simple Passion, & cela suppose encore plus évidemmēt quelque Effet dans la Substance qui connoist, ... les Idées sont absolument necessaires pour la Connoissance: Car soit que ce soit un Action ou une Passion, il faut necessairement qu'elle aye quelque Terme, & c'est ce qu'on appelle ordinairement *Idée, Verbe, ou parolle de l'Esprit*.[3]

What one knows when knowing is an idea which is a "Façon-d'Estre" of the soul. Such ideas arise in the soul because of the union with the body, upon movements of the body. And it is utterly impossible for the soul to know something which is not its own modification. The notion of vision in God is as naive as the natural prejudice that we need only open our eyes to see external objects[4]; Malebranche himself knows that we do not see external things, but only our own sensations. Hence, Foucher could not believe that Malebranche could make a similar mistake by offering ideas in God which would be as exterior – and hence as unknowable in themselves – as are the external things they supposedly make known.

Foucher's doubts in this matter are allayed by Malebranche's remarks concerning the sixth assumption. Foucher assures us, Malebranche says, "*que je me fonde sur ce que Monsieur Descartes a resolu touchant cette question. Cependant l'opinion de Monsieur Descartes est entierement differente de la mienne.*" [5] Thus is Foucher finally told point blank what, as Gouhier remarks, is "à peine perceptible dans la *Recherche: une philosophie nouvelle est née, qui prétend être autre chose que celle de Descartes.*" [6]

[1] *Ibid.*, 445.
[2] *Critique*, 116–119.
[3] *Ibid.*, 119–120.
[4] *Ibid.*, 122.
[5] Malebranche, *op. cit.*, II, 496–497.
[6] Gouhier, Henri. "La Première polémique de Malebranche," *Revue d'histoire de la philosophie*, I (1927), 35.

About the seventh assumption, Malebranche says that it was not his place yet to prove anything about extension; he was only combatting "les erreurs des sens au regard des qualitez sensibles." As for the problem of non-resembling representative ideas, Malebranche says, "je ne sçai pas comment il s'avise après *sept ans* de se plaindre d'une réponse de Monsieur Rohault. Il falloit le pousser lorsqu'il étoit vivant." [1] If Foucher had complained while Rohault was living, Malebranche is sure that Rohault could have settled the problem with only "deux ou trois paroles." Malebranche has nothing to say about it himself, however.

Foucher was not long in responding to this preface. A letter from Rene Ouvrard to Nicaise on 24 September 1675 describes the impatience with which Foucher awaited the publication of the second volume of the *Recherche*. Ouvrard remarks that he would hesitate to visit Foucher now, for "Je m'imagine qu'il ne voit voler devant ses yeux que des fantômes, des atôms et des idées, et qu'il n'y a point de machine dans M. Descartes dont il ne remue tous les ressorts." [2] Ouvrard sees no good in such critiques, but it is interesting to note that he considers what might be expected to be a violent attack upon Malebranche as an attack upon Descartes. Evidently Foucher was given the benefit of an advance copy, as volume two of the *Recherche* was officially printed on 28 September 1675. The first volume was printed on 2 May 1674. [3] The permission for the *Critique* is dated 10 December 1674. Foucher thus had six months to write and publish the *Critique*. The *Réponse pour la Critique a la Preface du second volume de la Recherche* took even less time; the permission is dated 31 December 1675, which means Foucher had only three months to get it ready after the appearance of the second volume of the *Recherche*. It was perhaps not too difficult, however, for Foucher repeats in the *Réponse* much that is in the *Critique*. The title makes one wonder how much Foucher was impressed by Malebranche's announcement that his was a new system of philosophy different from that of Descartes; the complete title includes . . . *où l'on examine le sentiment de M. Descartes touchant les idées*.

Foucher begins the *Réponse* by remarking that Malebranche should have answered the *Critique* wholly or not at all. Further, Foucher wants

[1] Malebranche, *op. cit.*, II, 497.

[2] Letter of Ouvrard to Nicaise (24 septembre 1675) in: Cousin, Victor, *Fragments philosophiques pour faire suite aux cours de l'histoire de la philosophie*, 4 volumes (Paris: Ladrange and Didier, 1847), III, 154–155.

[3] Malebranche, *op. cit.*, I, XXVII.

to stress that the *Critique* is meant to be a guide to errors made by many authors in the search for truth and is not meant to be a personal attack on Malebranche; the *Recherche* is only a touchstone. Foucher says that he does not mean that the assumptions cited are to be taken as Malebranche's complete method. However, any attempt to avoid error involves some method, and he still believes method should be one of the first things treated.[1]

Foucher proceeds as though Malebranche were a slow student. He carefully explains that all phantasms, sensations, and ideas are simple appearances which are nothing more than "nostre ame, disposées d'une telle, ou d'une telle maniere." He points out again that no proof has been given that our senses do not deceive us with respect to extension, figure, and movement as they do with color, light, heat, and other sensible qualities. The total difference the Cartesians stress between soul and body means that ideas – modifications of the soul – cannot possibly resemble extended things. Hence, it is impossible for such ideas to represent extended things.[2]

However, Foucher retracts his attribution of the fifth assumption to Malebranche since Malebranche says that ideas are not "*façons-d'estre de nostre ame*." Foucher says it is easy to see how he made the mistake. In the first chapter of the *Recherche* Malebranche says that ideas and sentiments are to our souls as figure and configurations are to matter. When Malebranche went on to say that ideas were not modifications, Foucher thought this was a distinction from "*façons-d'estre*" in analogy to the distinction of figures from configurations. Malebranche further says that modifications are within us in Book III, Part II, Chapter I, so Foucher concluded that ideas are within us. Even granting Malebranche his correction that ideas are not modifications of the soul, and laying aside the question of how such things can correctly be called ideas, Foucher points out that Malebranche still says of them: (1) they are spiritual, (2) they are not substances, and (3) they are received in our soul. Foucher cannot see why this is not contradictory, for these spiritual things can only be modifications of some substance; if they are received in the soul it is difficult to understand how they are not modifications of it. There is nothing else they can be.[3]

As for the sixth assumption, Descartes wants extended things to be

---

[1] *Réponse pour le Critique à la Preface*, xiv, xx, 4, 6.
[2] *Ibid.*, 17–20, 26, 29, 42.
[3] *Ibid.*, 103–108. For further examination of this point, see Chapter VII.

represented by ideas which do not resemble these things; Malebranche cannot deny that he also purports to have non-resembling representative ideas, for example, in Book III, Chapter IV. Malebranche replies to this only that Foucher does not understand; Foucher says he should instead have given an explanation. As for the seventh assumption, Malebranche makes no attempt at all to explain why our senses do not deceive us about extension as they do about other sensible qualities.[1]

Foucher points out that if ideas were not "façons-d'estre" of our soul, they could not be known immediately; they would be external things.[2] But there is an easy proof that they are not external. An idea is something which is known by itself without representation. The only things which can be known by themselves are modifications of our soul. Hence it is contradictory to say that ideas can exist outside our soul; if they could they would not be knowable in themselves. Foucher's argument suggests that if one needs an external idea to know an external thing, one would need an infinite regress of intermediary ideas to know ideas. Foucher concludes his task of clarifying the concept of ideas by remarking that Malebranche in the *Recherche* is the only person he ever heard of who says that ideas are not "façons-d'estre de la ame." If his vision in God system of ideas is not entirely incomprehensible, it is at least the most obscure Foucher has ever heard of.[3]

By 1685 Malebranche and Foucher were having occasional meetings. How can we visualize these meetings? No understanding seems to have arisen from them. Perhaps we can see the two, scurrying away from one another in their robes, each refreshed and lightened by the encounter, in wonderment at the obtuseness of the other. Foucher expresses his belief that Malebranche's system of ideas is incomprehensible even after a personal interview on the subject. He reports to Leibniz that it seems to him that Malebranche's "opinion des idées qui ne point façons d'estre de l'âme, est insoustenable." [4] After ten years of occasional mettings, Foucher reports again in a letter of 28 April 1695 in almost the same words. However, he now stresses that Malebranche's theory is dangerous as well as unintelligible:

---

[1] *Ibid.*, 112–113.
[2] *Ibid.*, 107.
[3] *Ibid.*, 40–43.
[4] Letter of Foucher to Leibniz (1685?) in: *Die Philosophischen Schriften von Gottfried Wilhelm Leibniz*, Herausgegeben von C. J. Gerhardt, 7 volumes (Berlin: Weidmannsche, 1875), I, "Briefwechsel zwischen Leibniz und Foucher," 379.

Le Pere Malebranche a assurement l'esprit bon et penetrant, mais il est embarrassé dans son system des idées, qui ne sont pas des façons d'estre de nostre ame et sont hors de nous, et quand on luy demande comment il faut concevoir que nous ayons des perceptions de ces idées, qu'il veut estre hors de nous, il repond qu'il ne comprend pas comment cela se fait qu'il ne pense pas qu'on le puisse jamais comprendre; mais il entre par la dans un profond pyrrhonisme.[1]

Foucher believes that to say we cannot know how we know is close to saying that we cannot know; this is the extreme of dogmatic scepticism.

Foucher firmly believed that he had an influence on Malebranche's thought. In his letter of 8 December 1684 Foucher tells Leibniz that what led him to undertake the *Critique* was the fact that he had published his *Logique* more than a year before Malebranche published the *Recherche*.[2] When the third volume of the *Recherche* appeared, Foucher wrote to Leibniz (12 August 1678) that Malebranche now agrees with many things in the *Critique*, notably:

(1) en ce qu'il veut que nous ne connoissions pas par les sens qu'il y a des corps hors de nous, (2) en ce qu'il avoue dans un chapitre particulier que nous n'avions point d'idée claire de la nature de nostre ame.

Foucher pointedly adds, "Cela estant, jugez, Monsieur, des consequences qu'on en peut tirer contre sa philosophie." [3] It might be noted here that one conclusion Foucher does not draw is that it cannot be proved that there is something outside of us, only that it cannot be proved that its essence is that of Cartesian matter. In his letter of 26 April 1679 Foucher again mentions to Leibniz that Malebranche's third volume is different from the first two and that "il y paroist estre un peu Academicien." [4]

If Malebranche became more cautious in his use of the term idea, he certainly never became Academic enough to doubt his theory. Foucher is particularly struck by the fact that Malebranche now admits that "nous n'avons point d'idée de la nature de nostre ame." [5] That the nature of the soul is known to be spiritual is the first unproved assumption of which Foucher accused Malebranche. He believes that

---

[1] *Ibid.*, Foucher to Leibniz (Paris, 28 avril 1695), 422. Foucher altered the terminology of Sextus Empiricus. According to Sextus, Pyrrhonists have not yet found that they know anything, while Academic sceptics dogmatically assert that nothing can be known. Foucher called dogmatic sceptics Pyrrhonists, and referred to his own mitigated scepticism as Academic philosophy.
[2] *Ibid.*, Foucher to Leibniz (Paris, 8 december 1684), 377–378.
[3] *Ibid.*, Foucher to Leibniz (Paris, 12 aoust 1678), 375.
[4] *Ibid.*, Foucher to Leibniz (Paris, 26 avril 1679), 376.
[5] *Ibid.*

Malebranche's whole defective theory of ideas derives from this assumption.[1] Since Foucher believes that the merits of a philosophical system can be determined by examining the theory of ideas it incorporates, he stresses the importance of not beginning with an unproved assumption which will determine a perhaps erroneous theory of ideas. From the first, the Cartesian distinction of thought from extension makes knowledge of the external world by ideas impossible. Since Foucher believes that we can know only by way of ideas, and that ideas are "façons-d'estre" of our souls, the possibility of knowing the external world is destroyed if one assumes that its essence is extension and that thinking cannot contain anything of extension. The mistake is in believing that one knows the essences of spirit and matter. Foucher says that we do not, and further that determining such a question is one of the last things one should do in a philosophical system, not one of the first as do the Cartesians. Descartes sees how different extension seems to be from thinking, so jumps to the conclusion that thinking is the essence of the soul and extension the essence of the body. What he should do is suspend judgment until he sees the consequences of such assumptions. Foucher says that Descartes never mediated deeply on his notion of idea, for he perhaps suspected that he would have to give up his whole system if he did. It is not, after all, established that all extension is material nor that there cannot be some extension in our ideas.[2] Experience should not be denied; there is extension in our thoughts because we sense it. The problem is to determine what the essences of mind and matter are, given this fact. To deny this fact and to substitute ideas which supposedly represent extended things without resembling them is to go from the obvious to the absurd. Why deny the fact that we sense extension just as we sense color? Why arbitrarily divide the sensible qualities? Why – as Malebranche does – make ideas into external things which are as impossible to apprehend directly as are extended things for the Cartesians? To do so is to make it impossible to know external things, and this, for Foucher, is to fall into dogmatic scepticism.

Foucher could not break away, as Descartes had not, from the belief that the soul must be united in some way with what is known. For the Scholastics, knower and known share the form of the thing known. Both Foucher and Malebranche use the figure that the soul

---

[1] *Critique*, 20-23; *Réponse pour la Critique à la Preface*, 13-14, 80-82.

[2] *Critique*, 21, 44-50; Letter of Foucher to Leibniz (Paris, 30 mai 1691), Gerhardt, *op. cit.*, I, 397-399.

cannot go out to intercept things directly. Foucher takes this to mean that their essences cannot be known, for all we can know are modifications of the soul. Whatever can be known is in the soul, and therefore, not external. The only possible way out, Foucher says, is that somehow the substance of matter and soul are similar. Since we do not know their essences this is entirely possible. Malebranche clings to the Cartesian assertion that we know the essences of soul and body, claims Foucher, but also tries to adapt the Scholastic way of knowing external things. He makes ideas external, but still says that they are knowable in themselves, and that in knowing them our soul is united to them. Thus, in the vision in God, ideas are somehow united to the soul, yet are externally existing in God. This is contradictory. And even if it is a sharing, as in the Scholastic account which if not contradictory is at least mysterious, they are not shared by knower and known but only by knower and God. We know *ideas* because of the union, but the problem still remains of how they make us know exterior material things. In us and in God they must be spiritual, so cannot resemble the Cartesian material world. In offering such a solution, Malebranche cannot have clearly seen the real problem – the need to define a new relation of representation between ideas and things.

Foucher believes that Malebranche is on the right track. He says he is not writing against Malebranche, but to help him, for Malebranche does not attack the Academics, and even agrees with most of their principles.[1] And Foucher hails as a milestone Malebranche's eventual statement that we have no idea of the soul: this seems to leave the door open for a re-evaluation of essences and the bridging in new knowledge of the gap left by Cartesian dualism. Nevertheless, the solution Malebranche offers to the difficulties of the Cartesian way of ideas suffers from the same inadequacies as does the orthodox way. In making this clear, Foucher shows that so long as the Cartesian dualism is retained, any way of ideas based upon it will fail as a way of knowing. Malebranche may have meant to deny that representation must be resemblance, but Foucher takes him to place ideas aside as something other than modifications of the soul in large part to avoid the objection that ideas cannot be like material things. If they are neither mental nor material, neither substance nor modification, what, then, are they? In a Cartesian world – and Foucher cannot ever see Malebranche as outside this world – even Platonic essences are totally spiritual and thus completely unlike material things. Foucher points out that

[1] *Apologie*, 156.

Malebranche never explains how representation can take place without resemblance between the representation and what is represented. Malebranche's explanation that one knows material things by ideas outside the mind itself needs explanation.

If ideas which are *in* the mind cannot give us knowledge of external things, how could ideas *outside* the mind give us such knowledge? Leaving aside the question of whether external ideas resemble external things, if external ideas are required to know external material things, then *as external*, might not these ideas themselves require intermediaries to be known? This would lead to an infinite regress of external ideas. Thus, Foucher believes, the Malebranchian way of external ideas is even more chimerical than the abandoned Cartesian way. Malebranche simply adds complications, doubling defects while removing none.

On Cartesian grounds, all we can know directly are modifications of the mind, and (Foucher says) anything which does not resemble these mental modifications cannot be represented by them. This excludes not only material things and material modifications, but also Malebranchian ideas. The principle that resemblance is necessary for representation seems sufficient to Foucher for rejecting both the Cartesian and Malebranchian ways of ideas.

Foucher's criticisms are directed at vulnerable points in Malebranche's system. We have seen that Malebranche did not, and evidently could not, answer these criticisms satisfactorily. Foucher believed that the major theory of ideas in the first volume of the *Recherche* is Cartesian, and that Malebranche introduced the theory of the vision in God only after encountering the difficulties of the Cartesian view in the actual composition of this first volume. We must conclude that detailed analysis shows that Foucher was justified in this belief.

Malebranche's occasionalism was in part a response to the problems besetting Cartesian dualism with respect to interaction between mind and body. Foucher thought this system was contrary to the experienced fact of interaction, but concentrated his criticisms upon the Malebranchian way of ideas. We have shown how Foucher must have interpreted the first volume of the first edition of Malebranche's *Recherche* not so much to vindicate Foucher as to present what would be a plausible reading by any late 17th century philosopher versed in Cartesianism. Ideas must be modifications of the mind, for everything must be either mental or material, and either a substance or a modification. When Foucher finally saw that Malebranche intended for ideas to be entities outside the Cartesian ontological framework, he decided that Malebranche was simply talking nonsense. Foucher dismissed the theory as an exhibition of religious enthusiasm, and went on to criticize the Cartesian way of ideas which many of Malebranche's remarks seem to support. As we shall see later, Berkeley had a similar difficulty in attempting to introduce an entity outside Cartesian ontology, and it was not until Hume that the locks of substance and modification were broken. More orthodox Cartesians tried to solve their problems within the Cartesian framework, and it is to a consideration of these attempts that we now turn.

# CHAPTER V

# THE ORTHODOX (NON-OCCASIONALIST) CARTESIAN WAY OF IDEAS

Malebranche gave up the notion that interaction occurred between mind and body. Like Foucher, numerous Cartesians thought that this interaction was obvious and thus retained it in their expositions of Cartesianism. These philosophers who do not offer occasionalist solutions to Cartesian problems are referred to as orthodox Cartesians, though there is no insistence upon the term, orthodox. As a matter of fact, these philosophers did consider themselves to be orthodox expositors of Cartesianism in contrast to someone like Malebranche who went so far as to assert that he was not a strict Cartesian. However, the orthodox Cartesians could not retain all the principles which seemed to underlie Cartesianism. They retained the strict dualism between mind and matter, and thus could explain interaction only by dispensing with the causal likeness principle. Concurrently, in order to contend that mind could know matter which was utterly different from it, they also had to deny the epistemological likeness principle.

ROBERT DESGABETS [1] (1605?–1678) was a Benedictine whose only publications were an exposition of Descartes' explanation of transubstantiation, and a purported defence of Malebranche against Foucher.[2] His unpublished writings include 240 folio pages conceived as a supplement to the philosophy of Descartes.[3] In his polemic with Foucher, Desgabets does not so much defend Malebranche as give what he considers to be an orthodox exposition of Cartesianism. He accuses

[1] A study of Desgabets and many writings not published during his lifetime are found in: Lemaire, Paul, *Le Cartésianisme chez les Bénédictins. Dom Robert Desgabets son système, son influence et son école, d'après plusieurs manuscrits et des documents rares ou inédits* (Paris: Félix Alcan, 1901). See also: Bouillier, Francisque, *Histoire de la philosophie cartésienne*, 2 volumes (Paris: Durand, 1854).

[2] Desgabets, Robert. *Critique de la Critique de la Recherche de la vérité, où l'on découvre le chemin qui conduit aux connoissances solides. Pour servir de réponse à la Lettre d'un académicien* (Paris: Jean Du Puis, 1675). Hereafter referred to as *Critique de la Critique*.

[3] Quotations which follow from the *Supplément à la philosophie de M. Descartes* are taken from the many selections reproduced in Lemaire, *op. cit.*

Foucher of regressing to Scholasticism in his attempt to compress the distinction between sensations and ideas, pointing out that scepticism and Scholasticism both depend upon attributing sensible qualities to material things. But in stressing the distinctions basic to Cartesianism between mental and material modifications, and between ideas and sensations, Desgabets recognizes the force of Foucher's objections. If the causal and epistemological likeness principles are retained as a part of Cartesianism, then neither is interaction between body and mind nor knowledge of body by mind possible. Hence, Desgabets dispenses with the likeness principles. Interaction is presented as one of God's mysteries; the knowledge relationship is said to be dependent upon intentional resemblance of ideas to things known. Foucher insists that this relation turns out to be neither intentional in the Scholastic sense nor resemblance in the ordinary sense, so explains nothing.

Desgabets feels that Descartes over-extends the method of doubt. The natural light gives us intuitive knowledge of the natures of the soul, the body, and of their union. The essence of the soul is thinking; we are immediately aware of this upon having any thoughts. But we are equally aware of the essence of the body, which is extension. And in every thought that we have is contained the intuition that the thought is a modification of the mind and is caused by an entirely different substance, body; no one ever mistook one for the other. Further, all experience contains the intuition that soul and body are completely united in interaction. Descartes, then, should not – and in actuality cannot – cast doubt on the existence of body. In doing so he denies a further intuitive truth which is evident to anyone who meditates upon his thoughts. It is impossible not to know "que la chose à laquelle on pense est telle en elle-même hors la pensée, qu'elle est représentée par la pensée." [1] The logically first truth, and the base of all sciences is the following:

Toutes nos idées ou conceptions simples ont toujours hors de l'entendement un objet réel, qui est tel en lui-même qu'il est représenté par la pensée, et qui contient le degré d'être qu'on y aperçoit.[2]

Our knowledge of the existence of the external world, then, does not rest upon Divine Veracity, but upon the principle that our ideas give us certain knowledge of the world. We know this with intuitive certain-

[1] *Supplement* in Lemaire, *op. cit.*, 150.
[2] *Ibid.*, 197–198.

ty; nothing is more clear and distinct than this principle which Desgabets insists is – rather than the *cogito* – the foundation of Cartesianism.

The distinction between sensations and ideas is absolutely necessary to remove error from the natural sciences. Once it is realized that only ideas of figure, position, size, and motion of material things are representative, and that sensations represent nothing external, the Scholastics will have no reason to postulate occult powers, and the sceptics will have no variation of properties from which to construct paradoxes.[1]

In the *Critique de la Critique* Desgabets accuses Foucher of not being concerned with the search for truth; Foucher engages only in destructive criticism.[2] Foucher ignores the clear intuitive knowledge we have of the essences of mind and matter. He further ignores the intuitive certainty that ideas always represent their objects truly.[3] As for the interaction between body and soul, it is enough to remark that God is responsible for it.[4]

Desgabets admits that ideas and sensations are both caused by the action of material bodies upon the mind, but says this is no reason why ideas and sensations should both be representative.[5] It is a fact that ideas are and sensations are not. As for representations, it is indubitable that some sort of resemblance is necessary if an idea is to represent a material thing, but Desgabets denies that this need be a resemblance in essence or substance as Foucher demands. Rather, it is "ressemblance intentionnelle & non pas entitative." [6] He explains that

la ressemblance intentionelle ou de representation est tout d'un autre genre que la reele, & que quelque parfaite qu'elle soit on n'en peut tirer aucune consequence à un ressemblance d'estre ou de nature.[7]

Foucher argues that our ideas cannot represent material things because they do not resemble them, but Desgabets says that ideas need not "really" resemble their objects, ideas represent their objects in that they make them known. [8] He says that everyone is aware that we think directly, immediately, and truly of the things of which we think; we seldom think of ideas.[9]

Desgabets further detects an insidious danger in Foucher's argument

[1] *Ibid.*, 149, 178–179.
[2] *Critique de la Critique*, 6, 16, 27.
[3] *Ibid.*, 55.
[4] *Ibid.*, 96.
[5] *Ibid.*, 103.
[6] *Ibid.*, 115–117.
[7] *Ibid.*, 119–120.
[8] *Ibid.*, 121.
[9] *Ibid.*, 107.

concerning the equality of sensations and ideas. From such an argument, Foucher claims that since secondary qualities are modifications of the soul, so also must primary qualities be modifications of the soul. That is, secondary qualities are nothing more than sensations, so also must primary qualities be nothing more than ideas, mental modifications. When Foucher claims that nothing mental can (resemble or) represent anything material, he would seem to be on the slope toward idealism. But Desgabets fears worse than this. Foucher says that our knowledge of the natures of body and soul is obscure.[1] In suggesting that our ideas of extended things are nothing more than modifications of the soul, this Academic is suggesting that there is no distinction between body and soul, that they are perhaps both of the same substance, and (Desgabets fears) alas! this substance is material.[2] He sees in Foucher's objections to non-resembling representative ideas not only a persistence of a notion of representation deriving from the Scholastic belief that our sensations resemble real sensible qualities in external things, but also even more an argument calculated subtly to convince one that the soul is material. For the notion that an idea must resemble to represent, coupled with the indubitable intuitive truth that our ideas represent their objects as they really are, would inevitably lead to the conclusion that our soul is material like the objects our ideas represent.

Foucher, in denying the distinction between sensations and ideas, puts primary and secondary qualities once again (as had the Scholastics) in the same – possibly material – substance. Desgabets, by clearly stating the *difference* between sensations and ideas – that sensations do not give us knowledge of the properties of external things while ideas make these properties known without resembling them – still admits with Foucher that ideas and sensations both are mental modifications. But by insisting upon the notion of non-resembling representation, Desgabets feels that he preserves the profound distinction between body and soul, preserves true philosophy, and (incidently) religion.

Desgabets believes that Malebranche is as bound to the principle that likeness is necessary for representation as is Foucher. He considers Malebranchian ideas to be images which resemble their objects. He believes that Malebranche conceives pure intellection to be a process in which the soul observes spiritual images which resemble the material

[1] *Ibid.*, 12.
[2] *Ibid.*, 165.

images traced in the brain. Malebranche takes an idea to be a "milieu objectif" in which we see the object as one sees a man in looking at a portrait; Desgabets has correctly, he claims, shown that the idea is only a "milieu formel," that is, a thought, which makes the thing known without resembling it.[1] He agrees with Foucher that the theory of the vision in God is merely an expression of piety, dangerous when misunderstood.[2] However, Desgabets believes he has – unlike either the sceptical Foucher or the pious Malebranche – provided an adequate Cartesian way of ideas, the way of non-resembling representative ideas.

Foucher immediately prepared a reply to Desgabets, though it took him four years to find a publisher who would undertake a book which is the response to the critique of the critique of the *Recherche*. Foucher begins by asking the strongest of sceptical questions. What is the criterion of the criterion of certainty? Men of good faith, Desgabets says, intuitively know that their ideas truly represent things outside them. But, Foucher asks, cannot even men of good faith be deceived? How is one certain that intuition is non-deceptive? Certainly the many who believe that sensible qualities are in external things do so in good faith. Perhaps Desgabets himself is deceived in his intuitive truths.[3]

Further, Desgabets' general rule for the sciences – that our ideas represent objects as they are – assumes that the criterion of truth has been established; no arguments are given for this.[4] Beyond that, even though Desgabets says that the rule holds only for simple ideas, it is still the case that not even all simple ideas represent their objects truly. Desgabets' rule gives no criterion for distinguishing true from false ideas; who is to say that one who has a simple idea of a red square is wrong in believing that redness is a (secondary) quality of the chair? And who is to say that the insane do not see objects having the (primary) qualities they describe? All ideas are true in that they are what they are, Foucher agrees, but Desgabets fails to give a criterion for determining when ideas are true of the world. *The* criterion of truth is still to be found.[5]

Foucher is also puzzled as to how Desgabets distinguishes ideas from

1 *Ibid.*, 202–203.
2 *Ibid.*, 200–201.
3 Foucher, Simon. *Nouvelle dissertation sur la Recherche de la verité, contenant la Reponse à la Critique de la Critique de la Recherche de la verité, où l'on découvre les erreurs des dogmatistes, tant anciens que nouveaux, avec une discution particuliere du grand principe des cartesiens.* (Paris: Robert de la Caille, 1679), 30–31.
4 *Ibid.*, 53.
5 *Ibid.*, 71–88.

sensations. It is agreed that the sensible or secondary qualities are modifications of our soul; yet many men still believe that material things are colored. And all men still *see* things as both colored and extended. Desgabets says God would be a deceiver if there were not a world of extension outside us, but why would He be any more a deceiver if there were no extended world than He is because there is no colored world? Foucher cannot believe that it is not obvious to everyone that wherever colors and the other sensible qualities are, there also are extension and figure. Ideas of extension, then, are as much sensible qualities as are sensations of color.[1] One can conclude from our sensations and ideas that there is an external cause of them, but from these effects alone we can determine nothing about what this cause is in itself, call it body or call it soul. Desgabets is making an incredible claim when he asserts that God would be a deceiver if ideas were not of their objects, for the distinction between ideas and sensations is arbitrary.[2] If Foucher recognizes a danger in his contention that we do not know clearly the essences of mind and matter, it is only that impatient dogmatists may thereby be led to make assertions about them on insufficient evidence. He certainly is not advocating materialism, for he does not have enough evidence to make any positive claims about the essences of mind and matter.

As for Desgabets' non-resembling representative ideas, Foucher repeats that he still cannot comprehend how an idea can represent without being like the object it represents.[3] Foucher points to the ontological similarity of ideas and sensations in that they are both modifications of the soul. Desgabets' difference between them – that ideas represent and sensations do not – must be based in something which surmounts their equal ontological status. But he offers no such higher base. To state clearly that ideas make things known without resembling is no more than to repeat the Cartesian problem without solving it. [4] What must be done is to explicate this strange relation of making known without resembling. Desgabets seems to be suggesting some notion of intentional species when he speaks of "resemblance intentionelle," yet he gives no explication at all of his sense of intentional. And in saying that he considers this sort of resemblance to be "tout d'un autre genre que la reele," he admits that his sense of resemblance

[1] *Ibid.*, 42–46.
[2] *Ibid.*, 59.
[3] *Ibid.*, 34–35.
[4] *Ibid.*, 35.

is not *resemblance* at all. In fact, "resemblance intentionelle" seems to
be nothing more than a phrase equivalent to nonresembling representation. It is easy to understand what one means when one says that
a portrait represents a man; Foucher would like Desgabets' sense of
representation to be explained as clearly.[1]

Desgabets offers the basic orthodox Cartesian answer to Foucher's
objections. Interaction between mind and matter takes place because
God decrees it. Representation of material objects by ideas is non-
representative. Desgabets attempts to explain this sort of representation
by speaking of intentional resemblance, but he offers no explanation
of what this sort of resemblance can amount to. At one point he says
that after all, we see things, not ideas,[2] and for this has sometimes been
considered as a precursor of Reid. Despite his use of the term, however,
he does nothing at all toward developing an intentional realism, and
throughout stresses the need of representative ideas, even if he cannot
explain how they represent.

We shall now consider the answers of further orthodox Cartesians, and
Foucher's replies to them. In general it is a repetition of the debate
with Desgabets, and for that reason we shall consider them only
briefly. The one new element is that explanation by appeal to the
mysterious power of God is extended from covering the domain of
interaction to cover also the domain of knowledge. It is claimed that
non-resembling representation need not be explained for God assures
it. The orthodox Cartesians abandon the likeness principles in order
to retain strict dualism and interactionism, but they can conceive of
no metaphysical principles to repair the breaches in their system; they
are driven to dependence upon the God in the Cartesian machine.

Louis de La Forge, Jacques Rohault, Pierre-Sylvain Régis, Antoine
Le Grand, and Antoine Arnauld are all orthodox Cartesians in that
each retains the strict dualism between mind and matter, and concludes that ideas are representative without resembling their objects.
La Forge was a physiologist, Rohault an experimental physicist, Régis
a superb lecturer and teacher, Le Grand a widely read expositor, and
Arnauld a distinguished theologian and philosopher. Here we shall
see the full force of Foucher's criticisms, and how such criticisms,
striking to the heart of Cartesian metaphysics, hastened the downfall
of Cartesianism.

Louis de La Forge (1605?–1679?) collaborated with Clerselier in

---

[1] *Ibid.*, 33–40.
[2] Lemaire, *op. cit.*, 179.

publishing Descartes' *Traité de l'homme*, and in 1666 published his own *Traité de l'âme humaine*.[1] He stresses the contradictory nature of Scholastic species which are neither material nor immaterial, pointing out that in their immaterial aspect they cannot be emitted from a material thing, and that in their material aspect they cannot be received by the immaterial soul. The species or images become in Cartesian terms nothing more than the various motions of material things, sense organs, nerves, and animal spirits operative in the Cartesian perceptual mechanism.[2] These material motions do not resemble mental modifications.

The Scholastics believe, La Forge says, that resemblance is necessary for representation because they confuse material images (the material motions) with ideas, because men have a natural prejudice to believe that sensible qualities exist in things, and finally because the principle that nothing is in the understanding which has not first been in the senses leads to the mistaken belief that ideas must be like material things just as sensations are thought to be. Representation, for the Scholastics, means resemblance. To point out the inadequacy of such a notion, La Forge says that in such case mirrors must be said to know.

La Forge stresses that what is known directly and in itself is always modification of the mind.[3] He states that it would be a contradiction to say that ideas resemble material things,[4] but we *do* know material things by ideas.[5] How? La Forge's answer more or less amounts to defining his terms. Ideas are said to be in themselves "des formes, des modes, ou des façons de l'esprit, par la perception immédiate desquelles nous apercevons les choses qu'elles nous représentent." [6] He continues:

Que si l'on demande ici comment il est possible que des choses spirituelles, telles que sont nos idées ou les formes de nos pensées, nous puissent faire concevoir le corps et ses propriétés, avec lesquels elles n'ont aucun rapport de ressemblance, cela n'est pas sans difficulté; mais néanmoins vous ne devez pas douter de ce qui vient d'être dit, principalement si vous prenez

---

[1] La Forge, Louis de. *Traité de l'âme humaine, de ses facultés et fonctions et de son union avec le corps, d'après les principes de Descartes* (Paris: Girard, 1666). On La Forge see: Balz, Albert B. A., "Louis de La Forge and the Critique of Substantial Forms" in *Cartesian Studies* (New York: Columbia University Press, 1951); Bouillier, Francisque *Histoire de la philosophie cartésienne* (Paris: Durand, 1854); and Damiron, M. Ph., *Essai sur l'histoire de la philosophie en France, au XVIIe siècle* (Paris: Hachette, 1846).
[2] Balz, *op. cit.*, 86-87.
[3] *Ibid.*, 89.
[4] Damiron, *op. cit.*, II, 31.
[5] Balz, *op. cit.*, 91.
[6] *Traité de l'âme humaine*, 127; Quoted in Damiron, *op. cit.*, II, 40.

garde à deux choses: 1° que l'esprit étant une chose qui pense, sa nature est nécessairement telle qu'il peut par ses propres pensées se représenter toutes choses en lui; 2° que notre esprit est *divinæ quasi particula mentis*, et que Dieu ne pourroit pas connoître les corps, s'il étoit impossible que sa pensée, toute spirituelle qu'elle est, les lui pût représenter.[1]

Hence, it is the nature of ideas to represent without resembling, it is the nature of our spirit to know material things by its ideas, and that is the way God knows, too. It seems superfluous to add that nothing is impossible for God: He, Who is no deceiver, has made us this way.[2]

God assures the union between body and soul, thus establishing causal interaction. Since representation cannot be based upon resemblance, La Forge bases the natural symbolism of ideas which represent material things on the causal relation. However, it is true that even the Scholastic explanation says that material objects cause us to have ideas which make these objects known; and the Scholastic explanation goes on to tell how the representation is effected, though La Forge does not. La Forge also leaves to God the problem of how substances unlike one another can causally interact; he is reported to have been, at least in conversation, a complete occasionalist upon this point.[3]

However one solves the problem of causal interaction, the problem of representation remains. In defining an idea as that immediate object of perception by which we know external things, La Forge may be claiming that ideas have a primitive intentionality which needs no further explanation. It would seem, even, to be superfluous to point it out, for the only argument that can be given for it is that it occurs, and this should be obvious to everyone, if it does. The difficulty with such a notion, and it is a difficulty which La Forge sees,[4] is that it makes ideas themselves unnecessary. If all they do is mediate a knowledge of external things, if what we think about are material things and not ideas as Desgabets says, then why are ideas needed at all? If one can see things directly, an analogy might run, why look into a mirror, or more appropriately, through a window-pane? Such an elimination of ideas is, of course, impossible for La Forge since what we perceive are ideas and not material things. Representation can no more be *transparency* than it can be resemblance.

Foucher did not comment on La Forge's exposition, but he obviously would have demanded again an explanation of non-resembling repre-

---

[1] *Traité de l'âme humaine*, 130; Quoted in Damiron, *op. cit.*, II, 40.
[2] Balz, *op. cit.*, 91–93, 99.
[3] Bouillier, *op. cit.*, I, 503.
[4] Damiron, *op. cit.*, II, 458.

sentation. La Forge abandons the likeness principles, but has only God to fill the gaps. He was followed by Rohault in his dependence upon the explanatory force of God's hidden ways.

JACQUES ROHAULT [1] (1620–1672) was a leader in Cartesian affairs in France. He gave lectures in experimental physics which made him a famous man, and Foucher probably made his acquaintance at these lectures. Rohault's *Traite de physique* published in 1671, was a standard text for nearly 50 years.[2] The Newtonian, Samuel Clarke, thought it so good that rather than writing a Newtonian text he translated Rohault's into Latin, correcting it by adding footnotes from Newton.[3]

As an experimental physicist, Rohault stressed mechanical explanations. Careful thought about matter informs us that its essence is extension and that its essential properties are divisibility, figure, and impenetrability.[4] Hence, the real elements from which all things are made are small figured bodies. By actions of these bodies upon our sense organs, sensations and ideas arise by which we distinguish external bodies one from another. No further explanation is given of how this process takes place other than that it is the nature of our soul as formed by God to be so affected in interaction with the body.[5]

The Scholastic mistake of thinking that sensations resemble sensible qualities in external things comes from their belief "that it would be impossible for luminous or coloured Bodies to cause those Sensations in us which we feel, if there were not in them something very like what they cause us to feel, for, say they, nothing can give what it has not."[6] Rohault says that the simplest reflection will show this principle to be faulty. One need only consider the pain we feel when we are pricked with a needle to see that the needle can cause an effect which is nothing at all like anything in the needle. Where the notion of intentional species arose was in a Scholastic interpretation of Aristotle's theory of vision. This is that things impress images upon the air, which images continue to be impressed through the medium until they are impressed upon the eye where the soul observes them. As an explanation of how

[1] On Rohault see: Balz, Albert G. A., "Clerselier, 1614–1685 and Rohault 1620–1675" in *op. cit.*; Bouillier, *op. cit.*; Damiron, *op. cit.*; and Mouy, Paul, *Le développement de la physique cartésienne, 1646–1712* (Paris: J. Vrin, 1934).
[2] Rohault, Jacques. *Traité de physique* (Paris: V$^{ve}$ de C. Savreux, 1671).
[3] Rohault, Jacques. *Rohault's System of Natural Philosophy, Illustrated with Dr. Samuel Clarke's Notes taken mostly out of Sir Isaac Newton's Philosophy, With Additions.* Done into English by John Clarke. 2 volumes (London: James Knapton, 1723). Hereafter referred to as *System*.
[4] *System*, 23–24.
[5] *Ibid.*, 115, 118, 248.
[6] *Ibid.*, 119.

this takes place, Scholastics say that it occurs in the same manner as an image is reflected in a mirror. Rohault first says that Aristotle is not to be taken literally here. Then he says that it is harder to explain reflected images than direct images, so the mirror analogy can be no explanation. Finally, he appeals to experience. He assumes that at their source images would be as large as their objects, and that they would diminish in size in direct proportion to the distance they are from the eye. This would mean that we could not see images of things which were within a few yards of us, for these images would be too large. But we do see large things which are close to us, so the Scholastic theory of intentional species is absurd.[1]

Rohault's objection here seems to be based on a misunderstanding of the Scholastic position. His own theory of perception is that we outlined in Chapter II: material things are impressed upon the sense organs from which distinctive motions are transmitted along the nerves to the pineal gland; this causes sensations and ideas which are immaterial effects which do not resemble their material causes. Ideas represent "the *Place, Situation, Distance, Magnitude, Figure, Number,* and *the Motion or Rest* of such Objects," but sensations do not.[2]

Foucher asked Rohault – perhaps at one of Rohault's lectures – his standard question of why it is that extension is not in the mind if color is. Rohault first replied that we do not know extension by the senses. Foucher proceeded to show that if we know color by the senses, we must know extension by the senses also. Rohault disagreed; in response to Foucher's question of how then we do know extension, he said by reasoning from sensations of touch on different parts of the body. This either begs the question or implies that the soul is extended. Assuming that Rohault wishes neither of these consequences, Foucher expands upon the contention that extension, too, is a sensible quality. He believes that Rohault really means to say that the ideas – Foucher says sensations – of extension resemble primary qualities of bodies, while other sensations do not.[3] Foucher believes that if Rohault persists in such a distinction, he is implying that soul and body are capable of the same "façon-d'estre," and this destroys the Cartesian dualism.

Foucher could not have been impressed by Rohault's argument that material things can cause mental modifications which do not resemble their causes. This is just the point Foucher himself stressed in claiming

---

[1] *Ibid.*, 236–237.
[2] *Ibid.*, 245–246, 248.
[3] *Critique*, 64–66, 76–80. (Because of a pagination mistake there are no pages 67–75.)

that we can reason from the occurrence of ideas and sensations to the existence of some cause, but can say nothing of the essence of this cause. If the essence of anything is known here, it is the essence of sensations and ideas, not the essence of material or mental substance. Descartes himself says that we know directly only our ideas. Rohault would not have to appeal to the mysterious power of God to explain the interaction between mind and matter if he knew their true essences, for knowledge of how this interaction takes place would necessarily follow from knowledge of their essences.

Rohault says that there is no reason for assuming that ideas (effects) resemble anything in the objects which cause them any more than do our sensations.[1] Ideas need not resemble their objects to represent them. But, Foucher insisted, if Rohault truly understood a non-resembling representative relationship between ideas and their objects, he would not have to use – as he does – the unphilosophical recourse of insisting that ideas make their objects known without resembling them because that is the role assigned to them by God. Régis, the next orthodox Cartesian treated, clearly recognized the necessity of explicating a new representative relation in which ideas make their objects known but do not resemble them.

PIERRE-SYLVAIN RÉGIS [2] (1632–1707) was converted to Cartesianism by Rohault, and followed in his footsteps to become a highly successful lecturer and writer on Cartesian physics. He came to realize that non-resembling representative ideas are a necessary part of the Cartesian system, and like Rohault before him he found the causal and epistemological likeness principles to be in conflict with the more basic principles of the Cartesian dualism. Consequently, he examined in detail how causal interaction and knowing can take place between two substances. His conclusion is that while interaction between bodies can be explained by reason in the order of nature, interaction and knowing between spirit and body are events in the order of grace which can be "explained" (i. e., accepted) only by faith.

Ontologically, Régis recognizes only two kinds of substances which differ in essence, spiritual substance and material substance. God is not a substance for He takes no modifications. Among twelve self-evident metaphysical principles which are the foundation of all

---

[1] *System*, 14.
[2] On Régis see: Bouillier, *op. cit.*, Damiron, *op. cit.*, Mouy, *op. cit.*; and Fontenelle, Bernard le Bovier de. "Éloge de Régis" in *Oeuvres de Fontenelle*, (Paris: Jean-Francois Bastien, 1790), Tome VI.

certitude in metaphysics, logic, physics, and ethics,[1] four concerning the ontological framework of Cartesianism are quite important to our interpretation of Cartesian difficulties:

(1) *Que tout mode présuppose une substance dans laquelle il existe.*

(2) *Que les modes sont tellement attachez à la substance dont ils sont modes, qu'il est impossible qu'ils deviennent jamais les modes d'une autre substance.*

(3) *Que tout ce qui existe, est une substance ou un mode.*

(4) *Que les essences des choses sont indivisibles, & qu'on n'y peut rien ajoûter ni diminuer sans les détruire.*[2]

From these four principles, several important conclusions follow for orthodox Cartesianism. Since mind and matter differ completely in essence (and their essences are clearly and distinctly known), nothing can be added to either of them which is like the other. Not only is it impossible for modifications of mind to modify matter, and vice versa, but it is impossible for modifications of either to resemble modifications of the other. And of key importance is the axiom that whatever exists is either a substance or a modification. Ideas can *only* be modifications of the mind; any attempt to make them into something outside the all-inclusive ontological framework of substance and modification as Malebranche (and later Berkeley) did, is ruled out from the start. The final conclusion is that ideas for Régis must necessarily be modifications of the mind which represent material objects without resembling them.

---

[1] Régis believes that his *Système de philosophie, contenant la logique, la métaphysique, la physique et la morale*, 3 volumes (Lyon: Denys Thierry, 1690), is one of the first and most complete of its kind. *"Nous entendons par* SYSTEME," he says, "non une seule hypothèse, mais un amas de plusieurs hypothèses dépéndantes les unes des autres, & tellement liées avec les premieres vérités qu'elles en soient comme des suites & des dépendances necessaires." (*Système*, I, 275-276.) Régis provides an entire interrelated system of philosophy. He begins with logic which treats of self-evident principles. His metaphysics is derived from these logical principles. Then the physics is grounded in the truths of metaphysics, and finally his moral philosophy is derived from the truths of physics:

Ainsi la Morale suppose la Physique; la Physique suppose la Métaphysique; & la Métaphysique la Logique: & par ce moyen toutes les parties de la Philosophie ont un tel rapport, & une telle liaison ensemble, que j'ay crû que le tout que résulte de leur assemblage, pouvoit justement estre appellé *le Système général de la Philosophie.*

C'est par ce Système qu'on pourra réduire les verités les plus éloignées aux premiers principes. (*Système*, I, [x].)

Régis thus sees all knowledge as comprehended in one complete system. One can have certain knowledge, and contrary to Mouy's interpretation (*op. cit.*, 166), Régis' physics is not probabilistic, but only problematic. He is a true rationalistic physicist. See my article, "A Note on the Probabilistic Physics of Régis," *Archives internationales d'histoire des sciences*, N° 66, 1964, pp. 33-36.

[2] Régis, Pierre-Sylvain. *Système de philosophie, contenant la logique, la métaphysique, la physique et la morale*, 3 volumes (Lyon: Denys Thierry, 1690), I, 73-74. Hereafter referred to as *Système.*

In further principles Régis stresses that we know only by way of ideas:

(5) *Que je ne connois les choses qui sont hors de moy que par des idées, & que les choses dont je n'ay point d'idées, sont à l'égard de ma connoissance, comme si elles n'estoient pas du tout.*

He bases the representative relation (as does La Forge) on the causal relationship between material objects and their ideas:

(6) *Que toutes les idées, quant à la propriété de représenter, dépendent de leurs objets comme de leurs causes exemplaires.*
(7) *Que la cause exemplaire des idées doit contenir formellement toutes les perfections que les idées représentent.*[1]

Régis reports that sensations do not represent external things, but only guide us in actions of self-interest, while ideas truly represent their objects.

In explicating principle (6), that their objects are exemplary causes of ideas, Régis compares ideas to paintings. He does not do this in order to suggest that ideas are images[2]; the comparison is made to stress a broad causal analogy. Paintings and ideas are both representative beings. Just as in painting there is the painter, the model, the brush strokes, and the canvas, so also in the production of ideas: God is the first efficient cause, the material things are the exemplary causes, and the soul is the material cause.[3] But here, unlike the cause of the painting where model and canvas are both extended, the material thing is extended while the soul is an unextended "material cause." Régis' analogy serves only to accentuate the fact that there can be no resemblance between an idea and its extended exemplary cause. Although he stresses as a self-evident principle that the exemplary causes

---

[1] *Ibid.*, 77.
[2] Mouy, *op. cit.*, 148–149, thinks it does.
In explaining how complex ideas are composed of simple ones, Régis points out that one must be careful to determine if complex
  idées sont véritablement claires toutes les fois qu'elles paroissent l'estre. ... car une idée peut estre composée d'un si grand nombre d'autres idées que l'esprit n'aura pas assez d'étendüe pour les embrasser toutes à la fois; c'est ce que l'expérience fait voir en une figure de mille côtez, l'idée de laquelle ne nous représente pas plus clairement cette figure qu'un autre figure d'un nombre de côtez différent (*Système*, I, 49).
Mouy takes this passage to mean that Régis does not distinguish ideas from pictorial images, but this is clearly not Régis' meaning. For Régis, the division between simple and complex ideas is made on what the soul can understand in a single action. Ideas of simple geometric figures can be, but ideas of complex geometric figures composed of simple ones cannot be understood in a single action, but must be pondered over. Another example Régis might accept would be that of the simple idea of a wheel compared to the complex idea of a clock.
[3] *Système*, I, 180–181.

of ideas must contain *"formellement toutes les perfections que les idées représentent,"* he does not go on – as do the Scholastics – to explain by reason as a part of the order of nature how ideas represent these perfections.

Régis says that knowing external objects by way of non-resembling representative ideas, and causal interaction between spirit and body, are not to be explained by reason in the order of nature at all; such events belong to the order of grace and are to be "explained" only in the sense that they are to be accepted on faith. Régis' unique interpretation of the facts of the Cartesian dualism is as follows: Man is an accidental union of spirit and body, and only in this union is a spirit a *soul.* That such union is possible is of the essence of neither spirit nor body, and it pertains only by the grace of God. While in this union, the *soul* always has the idea of extension. Particular brain movements always give rise to particular sensations and ideas of objects affecting the brain. All the *soul's* ideas, even of God, depend upon brain movements. Pleasure and pain lead men to love or hate, pursue or flee, objects of ideas for self-preservation. After separation of spirit and body, i.e., death, spirit has no longer the idea of extension, imagination nor memory of, nor power over the material world. Spirit can know and love only itself and God.[1]

This is Régis' "explanation" of events which belong to the order of grace. It is a description of events which are inexplicable by reason, but which do occur, and which can be accepted only on faith. Even the "reasonable" statement that spirit has the idea of extension only when in union with body is not offered as an explanation by reason, for we still do not know *why* this should be the case, nor *how* unextended spirit has the idea of extension. If anyone wonders how sensations and ideas are caused when material objects act on bodies united to spirits, and how ideas represent material objects, Régis' reply is that we cannot know these things, not simply because our knowledge is limited, but because the question itself rests on the mistaken assumption that one can explain these things by reason. The consequences of the union of spirit and body do not belong to the order of nature, but to the order of grace; what one knows about them is that they occur, and that their "explanation" rests on faith, not reason, Régis believes, then, that there is no conflict between reason and faith, because the independent princi-

[1] *Ibid.,* 112–133.
Régis, Pierre-Sylvain. *L'Usage de la raison et de la foy, ou l'accord de la foy et de la raison* (Paris: Jean Cusson, 1704), 1–10. Referred to hereafter as *L'Usage.*

ples of each apply only to the non-overlapping orders of nature and of grace. Scholastics and Cartesians alike have a tendency to attempt to explain events in the order of grace with the principles of reason, and events in the order of nature with the principles of faith, but neither is possible.[1]

Beyond the fact that they try to explain matters of grace with reason, Régis traces the Scholastic mistake of attributing sensible qualities to material things to the fact that sensations and ideas have a common cause in these material things. When one says, for example, "je vois cet homme," one is led to think mistakenly that his sensations are of a material thing as it is. However, material things are never sensed; what actually occurs in such situations is that one sees colors (that is, has sensations of color), and at the same time has ideas of a certain figure. Considered separately, ideas and sensations are seen for what they are; the Scholastic mistake comes from not considering ideas as such, but as including in their conception the judgment that sensible qualities (because sensations are caused by the same objects at the same time) belong to the objects of which one is concurrently having ideas.[2]

Du Hamel attacks Régis' exposition concerning ideas by pointing out that Régis' use of the painting analogy is grossly misleading, for the major purpose of the analogy should be to show not how an idea is caused, but how it represents its object.[3] Du Hamel gets the impression that Régis is saying that Cartesian ideas must be like their objects without being like them, and of course this is contradictory.[4] At least the Scholastic explanation of resembling species makes it intelligible how we know things, Du Hamel says. Even if this explanation may be incorrect in detail, it is correct in stressing that resemblance is necessary for representation. Hence, Du Hamel dismisses as unintelligible the notion that ideas can represent without resembling. (Of course, Régis' point simply is that it is unintelligible.) Du Hamel reiterates Foucher's objections, and then adds a new argument. We can never know for certain that our ideas represent material things unless we can compare them with these things. But on Cartesian principles we can know only ideas directly, and material things only through the mediation of ideas; hence, this comparison is impossible.

---

[1] *L'Usage*, vi–vii, 90–95.
[2] *Système*, I, 162–163.
[3] Du Hamel, Jean. *Réflexions critiques sur le système cartésien de la philosophie de Mr. Régis* (Paris: E. Couterot, 1692), 33–35.
[4] *Ibid.*, 27–28.

Even if it is the case that external things cause our ideas, we can still never compare the cause with the effect. Régis further claims that one can tell the difference between substances by examining our ideas, for example, of thinking and extension. But this is clearly impossible since our ideas are strictly modes of thinking which can be compared only with other modes of thinking, that is, other ideas. On Cartesian principles one can never know directly either body or soul, so can never be certain that we have knowledge of external things. Du Hamel concludes that all this shows Cartesianism to be absurd, for obviously we do know external things.[1]

In replying to Du Hamel, Régis explicitly rejects what he takes to be the Scholastic likeness principles. He expands this rejection by stating that ideas are neither formal nor objective images of their objects. Since Du Hamel insists that the Cartesians explain the notion of representation which allows them to judge of external objects by internal, non-resembling ideas, Régis offers the following: 1) It is the case that we know things only by ideas. 2) Our ideas do not resemble their objects. 3) Therefore, ideas represent by making their objects known. This is all. It is the nature of ideas to make things known and it is the nature of our soul to know. To ask for any explanation further would be like asking how light makes us see; that is, have sensations of brightness and color. The point is that sensations and ideas are known in themselves as what they are.[2]

But, of course, in shifting the problem, Régis raises another difficulty. It *is* an embarrassment for the Cartesians to explain how light, that is, the motion or "pression" of particles of matter, or ultimately motions in the pineal gland, can cause sensations which are modifications of the soul. Ideas are caused the same way, and even if one could bridge the causal gap, the queston still remains of how it is that ideas represent their objects. All Régis can say is that in knowing ideas we know them in themselves, and part of what we know is that ideas represent their objects. (Concurrently, in knowing sensations in themselves, part of what we know is that they do not represent objects.) There is no explanation by reason of these experienced facts; Régis says all we can do is accept them on faith.

Du Hamel has the final word. He repeats Régis' answer to the request for an exact explanation of non-resembling representation: It is

---

[1] *Ibid.*, 30–41.
[2] Régis, Pierre-Sylvain. *Réponse aux Réflexions critiques de M. Du Hamel sur le système cartésien de la philosophie de M. Régis* (Paris: J. Cusson, 1692), 8–11.

the nature of ideas to make things known, and it is the nature of the soul to know things by ideas. This, sighs Du Hamel, is a remarkable discovery for which all schools no doubt will be eternally grateful to the Cartesians. It is, however, hardly the proper principle on which to base a system of philosophy.[1]

We shall now consider another Cartesian who did give an explanation. Le Grand tried to show how non-resembling ideas could make their objects known by acting as signs.

ANTOINE LE GRAND (1620?-1699)[2] published *An Entire Body of Philosophy*[3] in 1694 in which he reduced the Cartesian system to a "Scholastic" scheme, that is, he presented a Cartesian scheme of hierarchial concepts for understanding the world. This work is the last major exposition of Cartesianism, and along with the publication of the last enlarged edition of Malebranche's *Recherche* in 1712 (it was actually completed in 1699) heralds the close of the Cartesian era.

Le Grand, like Arnauld, develops more than do the other orthodox Cartesians the notion that ideas have a double aspect. He says that

in the *Idea* or notion of a Thing two things are to be consider'd: *First,* that it is a Modus inherent in the *Mind,* from whence it proceeds; The *other,* that it shows or represents something. The former of these proceeds from the *Mind,* as its effective Principle; the latter from the *Object,* or thing apprehended, as from its Exemplary cause.[4]

The representative aspect of an idea is expressible in words as a proposition which reports the results of simple apprehension; it is not a judgment. All ideas represent possible existents, and only through judgment that they represent things that actually exist can error arise.[5]

Le Grand makes it clear that while ideas are spoken of as "Images of things,"[6] this is in no way a picture imagery; it is a conceptual imagery, that is, an understanding of the essences of things. For

[1] Du Hamel, Jean. *Lettre de Monsieur Du Hamel, Ancien Professeur de Philosophie de l'Université de Paris, pour servir de Replique à Monsieur Régis* (Paris: publisher unknown, 1699), 16.
[2] On Le Grand see: Bouillier, *op. cit.*; Lee, Sidney, *Dictionary of National Biography* (New York: Macmillan 1909); and *Nouvelle biographie générale depuis les temps les plus reculés jusqu'a nos jours* (Paris: Firmin Didot Frères, Fils et Cⁱᵉ, 1859).
[3] Le Grand, Antoine, *An Entire Body of Philosophy, According to the Principles of the Famous Renate des Cartes, in three Books*: I. *The Institution,*... II. *The History of Nature,*... III. *A Dissertation of the Want of Sense and Knowledge in Brute Animals,*... (London: Samuel Roycraft, 1694).
[4] *Ibid.,* Book I, 1-2.
[5] *Ibid.,* 9-10.
[6] *Ibid.,* 1.

the *Ideas* ... which we have of Things ... are *Conceptions*, or rather the Things themselves conceived and understood by the *Mind;* by which Intellection things are said to be Objectively in the *Intellect*.[1]

We can, for example, have no picture of God or spiritual things, but we can have ideas of them. And of those material things which can be pictured in their own realm, it is impossible to picture them with a non-extended substance such as the mind.[2]

Le Grand explains non-resembling representation by ideas of material things with the relation of substitution. He says that

*Relation* is nothing else, but a Mode of our Understanding, comparing one thing with others, because of some Properties or Acts that are found in them.

The relation of substitution

is that which intervenes betwixt the Sign, and that which is signified by it; the Measure and the thing Measured; the Image and the Original.[3]

There seems to be no place here for a relation in which a thing is made known without being resembled. One can compare two things, both of which have material properties, and one can compare two things, one of which is material and the other of which is mental, in the sense of measuring or imaging one by another.

The relation of making known must be that between sign and what is signified. But in saying this, Le Grand does as do the other orthodox Cartesians; he states the problem, offering this statement as a solution. For the sign has nothing to do with making what is signified known. Once the thing is known, Foucher would agree, a sign can be established or recognized for it, but original knowledge could not be attained by way of such a sign. And for a Cartesian there is no possibility of comparing sign with what is signified, no relation "of some Properties or Acts that are found in them" to allow one to recognize that this is a sign of that. Natural signs do exist – lightning is the sign of thunder – but in such case it is tantamount that both lightning and thunder have been observed. But ideas must ever be (upon Cartesian principles) signs of the sort as are mysterious comets, the portent of which is unknown. The Cartesians know the signs (ideas), but never what they are signs of. To learn that ideas are the signs of certain particular material things, one would have to observe the signs and

[1] *Ibid.,* 22.
[2] *Ibid.,* 9.
[3] *Ibid.,* 17.

the things in conjunction; but by the very nature of the case all that is ever observed are the signs, never the signified.

Le Grand's major causal axioms also make it difficult to determine the relation. "A Cause cannot give that which it hath not" is matched with "No Effect exceeds the virtue of its Cause." [1] From these principles one could argue that ideas cannot be the effects of material causes, for ideas are completely unlike material things. Because of this complete unlikeness in fact, it would seem to be impossible for the two to be in any relation whatsoever, let alone a causal one.

Le Grand says that the essential difference between sensations and ideas is that ideas are understandings, while sensations are not. Ideas can also be general, while sensations are always particular. [2]

The representative aspect of ideas is separated as propositional by Le Grand from the ontological aspect of ideas which is their being as modes of mental substance. He makes this distinction explicit in saying that besides ordinary ideas there are also

Propositions of *Eternal Truth*; which are not understood as Existing things, or the Modes of things; but as Eternal Truths abiding in our Understanding: As, *That which is, whilst it is, cannot be nothing*; *I am, because I think*; *What is once done, cannot be undone*; which are therefore called Common Notions, because they are so simple and clear, that they cannot but be perceived by all Men. Neither must it be look'd upon as an Absurdity, that we call any thing *Eternal* and *Immutable*, besides GOD; because we do not speak here of Existing things, but only of Notions and Axioms which are in our Mind. [3]

These notions and axioms enjoy a peculiar status in the Cartesian ontological framework. In Le Grand's genealogy of everything in the world, each thing represented is either a substance or a modification of a substance. [4] However, axioms and notions are not "Existing things" but are only "in our Mind" and ultimately in God's mind. Le Grand might have gone on to say that the representative aspect of all ideas is only in the mind, while their other aspect is their existence as modifications of the mind. (These modifications, by the way, he consistently conceives of as acts or actions of mind in consequence of their being modifications of an active thinking substance.) But having suggested an element (as did Malebranche) which has no place in the Cartesian ontological framework, Le Grand finds no way of classifying it. In his diatribe against Scholastic intentional species which some

[1] *Ibid.*, 50.
[2] *Ibid.*, 326.
[3] *Ibid.*, 15.
[4] *Ibid.*, 18–19.

Peripatetics said were neither material nor spiritual, Le Grand ridicules the notion that they could have any role in the perceptual process. More likely they are nothing at all. He forgets himself so far as to ask (supposing they were not material) "how can they represent *Extended Beings*, being without *Extension* themselves?" [1] As a matter of fact, ideas which are modifications of the mind *do* represent extended things without being extended themselves. The Scholastic prejudice, says Le Grand, that the cause must be like the effect is as absurd as to reason that the Earth must be a fiddler because it produces fiddlers. Ideas and sensations need not be like the motions which produce them, nor need ideas be like the material things they represent. [2]

As for explaining non-resembling representations, Le Grand says that just as we designate significance to words, "Why may not *Nature* as well appoint a Sign" which has no resemblance to what it represents? [3] That is, nothing can be transferred from material things to ideas, and no idea can be a similitude of material things, but God could so arrange it that material things do cause ideas which represent these material things. These ideas would be innate in the mind, arising due to the occurrence of certain motions in the pineal gland. Thus Le Grand, the last great expositor of Cartesianism, follows the other orthodox Cartesians in resting non-resembling representation upon the will of God. God can and does support such representation, but no explanation is forthcoming as to how he does it. Le Grand suggests the possibility that ideas are outside the Cartesian ontological framework completely (and thus perhaps not susceptible to the objections we have raised), but he reserves this status for Eternal Truths which are said to be in the mind. Ultimately they reside, without being, in the mind of God. According to Le Grand's own principles, if they have no being, they are nothing; and if they are in the mind of God with being, they could be there only as modifications.

We have now traced the development of the orthodox Cartesian way of ideas from Rohault to Le Grand. These philosophers all try to avoid sceptical criticisms of Cartesianism by denying the principles that likeness is required between cause and effect, and between knower and known. None of them find an intelligible substitute for the explanatory nature of these principles, so all of them conclude by calling upon God to support interaction and a representative relation which

---

[1] *Ibid.*, 284.
[2] *Ibid.*, 140.
[3] *Ibid.*, 284.

are basically mysterious. Arnauld comes to the same general conclusion with his treatment of perceptions which are by nature representative. After looking at his position briefly, we shall examine the underlying causes and implications of the Cartesian failure to explicate a non-resembling sense of representation in Chapter VI.

ANTOINE ARNAULD [1] (1612–1694), the famous Jansenist, wrote the "Quatrièmes Objections" to Descartes' *Meditations*. Despite the fact that the traditional argument that Descartes' establishment of the criterion for true ideas is circular appears in these objections and became known as "Arnauld's circle," Arnauld's positive philosophical position is Cartesian. *La Logique, ou l'art de penser*[2] (which he wrote with Pierre Nicole) is derived from Descartes' *Regulae*, and in *Des vrayes et des fausses idées, contre ce qu'enseigne l'auteur de la Recherche de la vérité* [3] Arnauld cites Descartes throughout as authority against Malebranche. It was in this dispute with Malebranche over the nature of ideas that Arnauld presented his own orthodox Cartesian position concerning the nature and role of ideas.[4]

In direct opposition to Malebranche, Arnauld says that ideas are modifications of thinking substance or spirit, and not separately existing *êtres représentatifs*:

Je prends aussi pour la meme chose, l'*idée* d'un objet & la perception d'un objet. ...il est certain qu'il y a des *idées* prises en ce sens; & que ces idées sont ou des attributs, ou des modifications de notre ame.[5]

Elsewhere, Arnauld says that besides *modification de notre ame*, the terms *mode, maniere d'être de l'esprit, pensée, notion, modalité de l'esprit*, and *perception* are synonymous with the term *idée*.[6] Arnauld generally

---

[1] On Arnauld with respect to the issues concerning ideas see:
Church, Ralph W. *A Study in the Philosophy of Malebranche* (London: Unwin, 1931); Damiron, *op. cit.*; Delbos, Victor. "La controverse d'Arnauld et de Malebranche sur la nature et l'origine des idées" in *Etude de la philosophie de Malebranche* (Paris: Bloud & Gay, 1924); Kremer, Elmar J. *Malebranche and Arnauld: The Controversy Over the Nature of Ideas.* (New Haven: Yale University Ph.D. Dissertation, unpublished, 1961); Lovejoy, A. O. "'Representative Ideas' in Malebranche and Arnauld," *Mind* XXXII, no. 128, 1923, 449–464; and Malebranche, Nicolas. *Recueil de toutes les réponses du père Malebranche ... à M. Arnauld...* 4 volumes (Rotterdam: R. Leers, 1694).
[2] Arnauld, Antoine. *La Logique, ou l'art de penser* (Paris: C. Saureux, 1662).
[3] Arnauld, Antoine. *Des vrayes et des fausses idées, contre ce qu'enseigne l'auteur de la Recherche de la vérité* (Cologne: Nicolas Schouten, 1683).
[4] Kremer, *op. cit.*, treats the controversy between Malebranche and Arnauld in detail, concentrating on the problem of the way in which ideas are caused to be of their objects.
[5] Arnauld, Antoine. *Des vraies et des fausses idées ...* in *Oeuvres de Messire Antoine Arnauld, Docteur de la Maison et Société de Sorbonne* (Paris: Sigismond D'Arnay & Cie., 1780), XXXVIII, 198.
[6] *Ibid.*, 198, 199, 228, 335, 342;
Arnauld, Antoine. *Défense de M. Arnauld, Docteur de Sorbonne, contre la réponse au livre des*

speaks of these mental modifications as perceptions which are representative of their objects. He insists that "Penser, connoître, appercevoir, sont la même chose."[1] Obviously, such ideas cannot represent their objects by resembling them; this would lead to the damnable conclusion that the mind is material.[2] Hence, Arnauld is scandalized to find Malebranche holding to two principles:

*Que l'ame ne pouvoit appercevoir que les objets qui lui étoient présents, & que les corps ne lui pouvoient être présents que par de certains êtres représentatifs, appellés idées ou especes, qui tenoient leur place, leur étant semblables, & qui, au lieu d'eux étoient unis intimément à l'ame.*[3]

These two propositions are contradictory in two ways: first, because the only things which can be intimately united to the soul are modifications of the soul and these modifications cannot resemble material objects, and second, because representative beings which are not modifications of the soul and which resemble material objects cannot be intimately united to the soul. Arnauld argues persuasively that in the early parts of the *Recherche* Malebranche took ideas to be mental modifications, and only later shifted to the notion that they are separate representative beings.[4] Because of this shift, Malebranche makes the mistakes he does.

Arnauld traces the origin of Malebranche's non-modal representative ideas to a childhood prejudice: since in mirrors we supposedly see not objects themselves but only their images, we never see objects themselves but only their images. Since Malebranche adheres to the epistemological likeness principles, he must make these image-ideas into entities external to the mind. Arnauld's attack upon Malebranche is based upon the principle that only a modification of a substance can be united intimately with that substance. Since ideas are so united to minds, their representation of material objects cannot depend upon any resemblance to material objects. Arnauld believes

---

*vraies & des fausses idées* (Cologne: Nicolas Schouten, 1684). Reference cited in *Oeuvres, op. cit.*, XXXVIII, 383.

[1] *Des vraies et des fausses idées* ... in *Oeuvres, op. cit.*, 198.

[2] *Ibid.*, 193.

[3] *Ibid.*, 194.

[4] Foucher also, it will be recalled, found that Malebranche begins in the *Recherche* with a Cartesian notion of idea and then later shifts the meaning of the term without warning. See also Ch. IV. Damiron, *op. cit.*, 482, after outlining Arnauld's objections to Malebranche, says that if he were to give Foucher's objections he would just be repeating those of Arnauld. This is not entirely true. Though Arnauld believes that both sensations and ideas are mental modifications, he retains their essential difference which Foucher denies. Foucher's major criticism concerning the unexplained notion of non-resembling representative ideas holds against Arnauld as much as against any other Cartesian.

that Malebranche holds to the epistemological likeness principle because of a mistaken analogy to the material world. The way ideas represent is unique to ideas:

> Quand on dit que nos idées & nos perceptions (car je prends cela pour le même chose) nous représentent les choses que nous concevons, & en sont les images, c'est dans tout un autre sens, que lorsqu'on dit, que les tableaux représentent leurs originaux & en sont les images, ou que les paroles, prononcées ou ecrites, sont les images de nos pensées. Car, au regard des idées, cela veut dire que les choses que nous concevons sont *objectivement* dans notre esprit & dans nos pensée. Or cette *maniere d'être objectivement dans l'esprit*, est si particuliere à l'esprit & à la pensée, comme étant ce qui en fait particuliérement la nature, qu'en vain on chercheroit rien de semblable en tout ce qui n'est pas esprit & pensée. Et c'est comme j'ai déja remarqué, ce qui a brouillé toute cette matiere des *idées*, de ce qu'on a voulu expliquer, par des comparaisons prises de choses corporelles, la maniere dont les objets sont représentés par nos idées, quoiqu'il ne puisse y avoir sur cela aucun vrai rapport entre les corps & les esprits.[1]

Thus, there can be no explanation of the way ideas represent by analogy to the way pictures (by resembling) represent their objects. Arnauld says, in fact, that there is no explanation of how ideas represent at all. One should be satisfied to learn that it is the nature of spirit to think of material objects, i.e., to have ideas or perceptions of them. One of his rules in the search after truth is not to seek for reasons beyond natures.[2] Like the other orthodox Cartesians, Arnauld believes it is enough to point out that God made thinking beings capable of thinking of material objects.

Ideas themselves have two essential relations: they are called ideas with respect to the relation they have to the soul they modify, and perceptions with respect to the relation they have to the objects perceived.[3] Malebranche seems to believe, says Arnauld, that these two relations mean that there are two different entities, perceptions and separately existing representative ideas. This, Arnauld says, is not so; perceptions themselves are representative of external objects through a relationship to those objects established by God. Arnauld specifies this relation only negatively, and does not explain it (nor feel he needs to). He says explicitly that the relation is not of the sort which exists between the signs of language and their objects, but it is fair to suggest that for Arnauld ideas or perceptions are some sort of indicative

---

[1] *Des vraies et des fausses idées* ... in *Oeuvres, op. cit.*, 199.
[2] *Ibid.*, 181.
[3] *Ibid.*, 198.

signs. Certainly he is open to this interpretation when he speaks of sensations. Malebranche agrees with Arnauld that sensations are modifications of the mind, and also that this does not mean that the mind is colored when it is having a sensation of color. Similarly, Arnauld insists, perceptions of squares need not be square.[1] Perceptions can represent their objects without being like them, just as sensations indicate their objects without being like them.

Malebranche's external ideas which represent their objects by resembling them are both unnecessary and redundant, for one would have to have perceptions of them if they did exist. Arnauld says it is better to face the fact that perceptions are of material objects directly. Nevertheless, Arnauld concludes that such perceptions are representative in essence.[2] By taking the representative relationship for granted as established by God without trying to explain it, Arnauld joined the ranks of the other orthodox Cartesians who failed to meet the crucial challenge, i.e., the demand for a philosophical explanation of non-resembling representative ideas.

---

[1] *Ibid.*, 187, 309–313.
[2] *Ibid.*, 199.

# CHAPTER VI

# AN ANALYSIS OF THE CARTESIAN FAILURES
# TO SOLVE PROBLEMS FACING CARTESIANISM

Desgabets, La Forge, Rohault, Régis, Le Grand, and Arnauld have all been called orthodox Cartesians because they have the following in common:

(1) They keep the strict Cartesian dualism between the two created substances, mind which has as its essence or *is* active unextended *thinking*, and matter which has as its essence or *is* inert unthinking *extension*.[1]

(2) They insist that causal interaction takes place between these two substances, resulting in ideas and sensations; the ideas are representative of their material causes; the sensations are not.

(3) They agree that whatever has being must be either a substance or a modification of a substance.

Obviously, ideas which are modifications of active, unextended thinking cannot resemble inert, unthinking extension or its modifications. Thus, it logically follows that support for the orthodox Cartesian claim that ideas represent material objects cannot be based upon a relation of resemblance. Similarly, it follows that if there is causal interaction between mind and matter, such interaction cannot depend upon any sort of engagement – on the analogy of one gear with another – between like aspects of the two substances. In this way, the orthodox Cartesians find these three principles inconsistent with the likeness principles; therefore,

(4) They reject the principles that likeness is necessary between cause and effect, and that likeness is necessary between what represents and what is represented.

Foucher's objections are based upon an acceptance of these likeness

---

[1] I take the orthodox Cartesians to be equating essence with substance. Thinking, as the essence of mind, is the substance of mind, and not the essential attribute of mind. One could know essential attributes, as Locke says, without knowing the thing in itself; the Cartesians claimed to know the thing in itself.

principles, and upon the conviction that in any conflict of principles, a reasonable philosopher will abandon most other principles before abandoning the likeness principles. Even in the face of statements from them to the contrary, Foucher still contends that the orthodox Cartesians cannot really mean to give up the likeness principles; they are too basic to the explanations of the engagement between cause and effect, and of the representative aspect of ideas. Foucher could not understand how interaction between substances could be explained without there being some likeness between them. And representation seemed to him to be so dependent upon resemblance that the two terms were practically synonymous. Therefore, the essential difference the orthodox Cartesians insist upon precludes (according to Foucher) the possibility of interaction and representation which everyone experiences. It seemed much more reasonable to him to suppose that the orthodox Cartesians do not really know the true essences of mind and matter. If mind and matter *do* differ in essence, then, Foucher says, a new relation of non-resembling representation must be made plausible. We have seen that the long demanded explication was not forthcoming. Some of the inadequate attempts of the orthodox Cartesians to provide an explanation, and some of the reasons for the failures of these attempts are considered in the following. Specifically, we shall examine the notions of ideas as natural signs, mechanical causation, external ideas, and direct acquaintance. We shall conclude that Cartesians have trouble with each of these notions because of their (implicit) dependence upon the likeness principles and the ontology of substance and modification.

The orthodox Cartesian notion of *idea* must be examined closely. The distinctions between the faculty of the intellect which makes it possible for the mind to have ideas and the operation of this faculty, and between each of them and the object of this operation (if there are such distinctions) are not always clear. What does seem clear (this is expressed most strongly in Le Grand and Arnauld) is that ideas, being modifications of an active mind, are actions of the mind in contrast to the passive modifications of inert matter. There are four recognizable aspects of such ideas: they represent objects external to the mind; they are modifications of the mind; they differ from sensations; and they differ among themselves. The representative aspect could reasonably be thought to depend upon a causal relation between the object represented and the representing idea. Thus, the object could be considered to be both the exemplary and the efficient cause of the idea.

But, if the object is a *material* object, it can be neither. A material object cannot be an exemplary cause in the sense of being a model, archetype, or pattern of a mental idea, because there is no likeness between them. A material object cannot be an efficient cause of an idea, because the essential difference between mind and matter precludes the possibility of any conceivable interaction between them. (As will be discussed, the Cartesians are restricted to mechanical explanations of causation.) Nevertheless, the orthodox Cartesians are convinced that material objects somehow cause ideas, and in doing so cause those ideas to represent the said material objects. How this is done is not clear.

Ideas differ one from another and they represent different objects. It might be thought, therefore, that the aspect by which they are distinguished one from another is the same as the aspect by which they represent different objects. This would reduce the actual aspects of ideas to three. However, this conclusion cannot be drawn. Sensations are equal to ideas in being modifications of the mind which differ among themselves, but the aspect which allows us to distinguish them one from another is not a representative aspect, for sensations do not represent. Hence, if we identify in ideas the representative aspect with the aspect which allows us to distinguish ideas one from another, then ideas can no longer be distinguished from sensations. If there is to be a reduction of kinds of aspects of an idea by finding or making two of them to be identical, these two cannot be the aspect by which ideas are distinguished one from another and the aspect by which ideas represent objects external to the mind. They could be only the aspect by which ideas represent an object external to the mind and the aspect by which ideas differ from sensations. In fact, this is just what the Cartesians say: ideas differ from sensations by having representative aspect; sensations differ from ideas by lacking a representative aspect. (That is, sensations have only three aspects: they are modifications of the mind; they differ from ideas; and they differ among themselves.) Foucher's criticisms amount to pointing out that the orthodox Cartesians do not indicate what the representative aspect of ideas amounts to. Foucher would reduce the aspects of both ideas and sensations to two: they both are modifications of the mind which differ one from another, but ideas do not differ in any appreciable way from sensations. Since Foucher notices no *special* representative aspect, this is either that aspect by which ideas and sensations differ one from another (so they both are representative), or neither ideas nor sensations have any representative aspect at all. (Sensations, of course, can be signs. It will be shown immediately that the interpretation of representative ideas as signs is inadequate because the relation of signification is externally, arbitrarily imposed, and is not based on any representative aspect internal to the sign.)

The orthodox Cartesians say that ideas represent their object by making them known. They see that the representative aspect of ideas cannot be resemblance, and therefore agree that the picture analogy is misleading. The analogy to the way signs represent their objects is a possible alternative explanation of *making known*. The first step they take toward explicating representation in the sense of making known, then, is giving as examples signs such as words, mathematical symbols, and noises, all of which represent without resembling their objects. These signs represent both our ideas and external objects, yet resemble neither. Therefore, if the sign relation is understood, there should be no difficulty, say the orthodox Cartesians, in conceiving that ideas can in the same way represent without resembling. However, once the sign relationship *is* understood, it is seen to be of no help in explicating how ideas make their objects known. The relation between a sign and what it signifies is arbitrary. The sign 'sun' represents the idea we have of the sun because we can know the idea directly, and arbitrarily assign to it this sign. On the sign analogy, then, if the idea of the sun represents the real sun, we should have to know the sun apart from the idea in order to be able to assign the idea to it. But, of course, since material objects are not known directly, but only by way of ideas, it is contradictory to suppose that we can know material objects prior to assigning ideas to them in the direct way that we know ideas prior to assigning words to the ideas.

The orthodox Cartesian reply to this objection is that *God* assigns non-resembling ideas as signs of external objects. Now, one wants to know of ideas which make their objects known, how it is that we know through them *which* external objects they represent, and how we know that they *truly* represent their objects. The picture analogy offers an answer to the first question: a picture-idea pictures its object. But concerning the second question, recall a classic objection to the picture analogy: one cannot say how accurate a portrait is if one has never seen the model; similarly, one cannot assert that a picture-idea is an accurate representation of an object (or even that it is representative at all) unless one knows in some other way what the idea is meant to represent. *If* the orthodox Cartesians could accept the picture analogy (which they cannot because of the dualism), they might answer that what the picture-idea represents is guaranteed accurate by a non-deceiving God. But since they cannot use the picture analogy, whether and how the object represented is made known through our knowing a non-resembling idea are exactly the questions at issue.

Consider again how it is that a sign signifies its objects. It does this not through any special internal representative aspect (as does a picture-idea,) but through an arbitrary external relation. Before knowing which idea a word represents in the sense of signifies (e.g., a word representing the idea of an animal one has never seen), one must have known directly an idea which is at least similar to that the word represents. (Obviously, the analogy here is only to words which *do* represent.) In the same way, if one is to know what his ideas represent, one must (on the sign analogy) have known directly an external object at least similar to that the sign-idea represents; but, it is impossible on Cartesian principles to know *any* external object directly. Hence, though a non-deceiving God might assure us that sign-ideas are *signs*, this would not help us in knowing of which and what objects they are signs. We still would not know what the sign-ideas represent unless we knew the external objects directly. Another way of putting this point is that on the picture analogy, ideas have content or connotation as well as reference or denotation; on the sign analogy, ideas have only reference or denotation. God might assure us that the connotation of a *picture*-idea is correct without showing us the represented object, but it is difficult to see how He could assure us of the denotation of a *sign*-idea without showing us the signified object. This way of making the point also brings out a possible further inadequacy of the sign analogy. The Cartesians wish to speak of the truth or accuracy of ideas; it is not usual to speak of a sign's being true to its object. One could make sense of this by speaking of systems of signs organized with formation rules and type-levels. God's assurance, then, would amount to guaranteeing that the relations pertaining among the signs were true of the relations pertaining among the objects. But even here, we would not know *what* the objects in themselves are. (And, as a matter of fact, such a possibility is really only a variant of the rejected picture theory.)

Hence, our conclusion must stand: While the picture analogy is misleading, the sign or language analogy is subtly even more so. For though it is perfectly true that we can represent ideas with words which do not resemble them, to state this about ideas and external objects is beside the point if true. And, according to Cartesian principles, it is false. The difficulty is precisely that external objects are *not* known directly as ideas are. The problem is not how something non-resembling (e.g., a word) can represent what can be known directly (e.g., an idea), but how something non-resembling (e.g., an idea) can represent what can *not* be know directly (e.g., an external object). It is a mistake to think that non-resembling ideas can make external objects known in the way that signs signify their objects, for the relation standing between a sign and its object pertains only after the object is previously known; the object of an idea cannot be previously known. It seems clear, then, that if external objects are known only by way of representative ideas and never directly, these ideas cannot be sign-ideas, and the relation of representation cannot be that of signification.

The basic objection is similar to that of Sextus Empiricus on indicative signs.[1] The orthodox Cartesian response is a theory like that of the Stoic lecton theory: one knows that ideas make things known because one gets to know things by ideas.

In the end, the orthodox explanation of how non-resembling ideas represent their objects amounts to the claim that there is a primitive, indefinable relation of representation between ideas and the objects they make known. It is a fact about the way God made the world that ideas make external objects known. If someone objects that just as a man born blind cannot be told with words what the sensation of color is, so it would seem that a man who can never know objects directly cannot learn from ideas what external objects are, the orthodox Cartesians might agree. Such making known by ideas seems impossible, and certainly is inexplicable; nevertheless, it occurs, and is guaranteed by God Who is no deceiver. That mind knows body by non-resembling representative ideas is nothing short of miraculous. Foucher's last word in the controversy is the scornful reminder that expressions of faith in the infinite wisdom and incomprehensible ways of God cannot be substituted for metaphysical explanations.

The orthodox Cartesian explanation – or lack of it – leads to one final possibility. La Forge recognizes that non-resembling ideas which represent external objects in no way that we can understand may seem to be superfluous. Why could not God allow us to know external objects directly? Ideas then would be unnecessary, or if they were present, their representative aspect could be described as transparency. However, if the traditional way of mediate ideas is abandoned, and a

---

[1] Cf. Sextus Empiricus. *Against the Logicians* in Bury, R. G. *Sextus Empiricus with an English Translation*, (London: Wm. Heinemann, Ltd., 1935), II, 311 ff.

theory of direct perception substituted, all the sceptical problems the Cartesian theory of ideas is meant to avoid would return – as Thomas Reid was later to discover.

The orthodox Cartesians have a tendency to answer the question of how ideas represent material objects by making the statement that material objects obviously cause ideas, and for this reason ideas can represent them. Even if it were enough to point out that ideas represent material things because they are related to them as effect is to cause, causal interaction between mind and body stands in need of explanation. Such an explanation is not provided.

The only explanation of cause offered by the orthodox Cartesians is a sheerly mechanical one based on the impact of bodies in which the effect always resembles the cause. (The statement that God causes – i.e., creates – all things is not considered to be a philosophical explanation. Kemp Smith points out how the Cartesians improperly try to save themselves with causation in the sense of creation.) [1] The major causal axioms imply the causal likeness principle. Le Grand stated it as follows:

> A Cause cannot give that which it hath not.
> No Effect exceeds the virtue of its Cause.[2]

In the material world, all changes are caused by the impact on figured particles of extension by other such particles which are in motion. If the bumping particle loses motion, the bumped particle gains it. If the shape of either changes, the new indentation in the bumped, e.g., is matched either by a bulge on the other side or by internal adjustments on the same principle. Any seemingly new or different properties in the effect caused by the material thing are always explained as deriving from properties which must have existed imperceptively in the cause, or must be a direct consequence of the cause, explicable by mechanical laws of motion and impact.

Illustrations of this principle are numerous. One might not expect the phenomena of magnetism, for example, to be explained in mechanical terms. The Scholastics appealed to occult powers to explain it, and observation of such phenomena were among the reasons leading Leibniz to introduce forces into his New System. The Cartesian explanation of the phenomena of magnetism, however, is a striking *tour de*

[1] Smith, Norman Kemp. *Studies in the Cartesian Philosophy* (London: Macmillan, 1902), 229ff.

[2] Le Grand, Antoine. *An Entire Body of Philosophy ... Book I* (London: Samuel Roycroft, 1694), 50.

*force* in its adherence to mechanical principles. It is postulated that there are imperceptible pores with screw-like paths in loadstones. These pathways exactly match the twist of some of the tiny particles which are being continuously swept through the universe by subtle matter. When the right combination is made of pore and particle, the particles spiral out of the ends of the loadstone with a violent spin, turning to the right from one end, and to the left from the other. This means that there should be attraction between loadstones if the ends which accomodate similar twists are put together, and repulsion if ends accomodating opposite twists are put together. This attraction and repulsion is actually observed in experiments. Ordinary iron is attracted by either end of a loadstone because the pores in iron are in a general state of disorder. By keeping a piece of iron in contact with a loadstone, the violent motion of the spinning particles aligns the pores in the iron, turning it into a magnet.[1]

Such examples abound in the writings of the orthodox Cartesians. Chemical changes are also explained mechanically. The digestion of food and the growth of animals is viewed as nothing more than the breaking down and rearrangement of particles. Experiments with the microscope seemed to confirm such theories. For example, the box-within-box theory of animal generation seems both reasonable and mechanically possible to the Cartesians. Since matter is infinitely divisible, it is possible that all the trees which are ever to be the heredity of a single seed could easily be contained in miniature in that seed. Dissection shows that this is the case for the plant which is to grow imediately from the seed, so there is every reason to believe that with ever more powerful microscopes one could discover seeds within seeds within seeds.

In all the mechanical explanations of events in the material world, then, the effect is in some way like the cause. The very engagement of one thing with another – again on the analogy of one gear with another – depends upon the likeness between the two things. All causal inter-action is reducible to impact between material things, and all effects are seen to follow from their causes in a fashion which is ultimately as simple to understand as it is to understand how a seal makes an impression in wax.

The seal and wax example is significant. It is one of the more obvious examples used in applying the picture analogy to the way of ideas. In the Scholastic explanation of perception, also, the effect must be like

[1] *Ibid.*, 199.

the cause. Both of these explanations (the picture analogy and the Scholastic) open the possibility of interpreting the soul as being material like the material things it knows. If seal and wax are material, then would not mind similarly impressed by a material thing have to be material? And if the form of a thing can be shared (something Malebranche as well as the Scholastics suggest), would not the mind which shares the form with a material thing have to be like that material thing? We have seen that the orthodox Cartesians are quite aware of this danger. This is one reason they stress the utter difference between mind and matter, and hence that the ideas by which we know material things are not like the material things. And since these ideas are also said to be caused by material things, the Cartesians must stress that an effect need not be like its cause. The examples of causal interaction between unlike things, however, are limited. They reduce to the statement that the material world is an effect unlike God Who is its cause[1]; therefore, since causal interaction between unlike things occurs in this one case, it is possible for ideas to be caused by matter which is unlike them. But even this appeal to God's causing the material world cannot support the possibility of causal *interaction* between mind and matter (though it might support occasionalism). For God's causal activity is *creative*. God causes the material world in the sense that he creates it. Even though we may not understand this creative activity, we do understand it well enough to know that the causal relation evidently pertaining between matter and mind is not of the sort in which one substance creates another. Hence, though God's creative act is mysterious, the causal interaction between body and soul is even more mysterious. It is not natural, the orthodox Cartesian would agree, for an effect which is not the result of an act of creation to be unlike its cause, and to assert that it is would be to shake the foundations of mechanical physics. The only *understandable* explanation of casual interaction rests on the engagement made possible by the likeness between cause and effect.

Thus, the orthodox Cartesians not only must explain how non-resembling ideas can represent their objects, they must explain how these ideas can be caused by non-resembling causes. They can do neither on the only explanatory principles available – those of mechanical physics. Thus, they are reduced to asserting over and over again

---

[1] To any objection that no true cause can produce effects which do not resemble it, Régis, for example, replies that then "Dieu même ne seroit pas une véritable cause, parce que tous les effets qu'il produit, sont d'une nature différente de la sienne" (*Système*, I, 124).

that representation and interaction *do* happen, and that such phenomena are inexplicable only in the sense that they do not require explanation: God has ordained that such interaction and representation be.

Malebranche has been represented here, as is usual, as deviating from
the orthodox Cartesian position, though here not simply because he is
an occasionalist. After all, to an outsider, the inexplicable interaction
of the orthodox might not seem to differ significantly from Malebranche's assertion that it is only an appearance of interaction,
particularly since in both cases God is the supporting agent. Malebranche's radical innovation is in his treatment of ideas. Concerning
ideas he breaks not only with the Cartesian, but with the Scholastic
ontological tradition as well.

Malebranche met the problem about causal interaction by denying
that there is interaction between mind and matter. This seems to be
an immediate result of his adherence to the ontological dualism and the
causal likeness principle. It is because of the complete difference or
unlikeness between mind and matter that Malebranche insists that
they cannot interact. Even God, Who is certainly different from both
matter and finite mind, can interact with both only if He is essentially
mental, and because He contains matter eminently. The causal likeness principle seems to be thus preserved.[1] So while Malebranche
objected to the orthodox solution on the grounds that mind and matter
cannot interact, though God can interact with each of them, the orthodox Cartesians objected to occasionalism on the grounds that if God
can interact with substances completely different from Himself, He
can surely make it so that mind and matter can interact despite their
essential difference. It would require a breach of the causal likeness
principle, but it would be, they felt, less deceptive.

Malebranche's serious break with Cartesianism came over the all-
inclusive ontological type-distinction between substance and modification. It was an unsuccessful break, primarily because he did not see
fit to deny the causal and epistemological likeness principles, nor the
principle that direct acquaintance is necessary for knowledge. His
retention of the likeness principles is most evident in that he still insists
that the cause of an idea must have as much or more formal or eminent
reality as the idea has objective reality.

---

[1] Actually, the causal likeness principle is not preserved in the sense required. What
Malebranche shows is that any sense of effective causal interaction between two unlike
substances is meaningless. God *creates* mind and matter rather than causally interacting
with them. Hence, in substituting this creative "interaction" for causal interaction, Malebranche does not, after all, preserve the *causal* likeness principle.

Malebranche realized that on the Cartesian principle of the complete difference in essence between mind and matter, plus the likeness principles, it is impossible for Cartesian ideas to represent material objects. On these principles, no modification or action of the mind can *resemble* a material object, hence no idea which is a mental modification can *represent* a material object. Though Malebranche could deny that there is real interaction between mind and matter, explaining why it appears to us that there is such interaction, he could not very well deny that we have real knowledge of material objects, even though material objects are only the occasional causes of this knowledge. It would not do to explain that we only appear to have knowledge, for that would either be the same as having knowledge, or would not be an appearance of *having knowledge* at all. Therefore, he makes a bold move; he attempts to separate the idea from the modification or action of the mind. Malebranche said that ideas are *not* modifications of the mind, but are *in* God. God had to have ideas of the essences of material objects before He created material objects, and by sharing these ideas with us God allows us to have knowledge of material objects just as God Himself has knowledge of them.

Malebranche, particularly in his controversy with Arnauld, seems to believe he has said enough simply by saying that ideas are not modifications of our minds, but are *in* God. One might grant that if ideas are *in* the mind of God as they were thought to be in our minds, that is, as modifications, then they would be mental, and we could possibly know them on Cartesian principles. We might know modifications of God's mind by having ideas which resemble and hence represent those in God's mind. But, since God's ideas would be modifications of a presumably mental substance, one could ask how even *they* could resemble and hence represent *material* objects. Malebranche avoids this question by denying that ideas are modifications of God's mind. Not only are ideas not modifications of mind, ideas are not even mental!

Malebranche reaches this conclusion as follows: He stresses the distinction between ideas which represent and sensations which do not, explaining that the basis of this distinction lies in the fact that sensations are mental modifications whereas ideas are not. Obviously, mental modifications cannot represent (resemble) material objects, but, ideas *do* represent material objects. But does this mean that ideas are material? Even though it is implied that ideas resemble (since they represent) material objects, Malebranche surely denies that they are material. He seems to be suggesting that ideas are neither substances nor modifications of substances. But, what, then, are they? Malebranche retains the ontological type-distinction between substances and modifications of substances, but for a Cartesian this classification is all-inclusive. Whatever is, is either a substance or a modification. Malebranche must deny that the traditional Cartesian ontological categories are complete. Ideas appear to be some kind of third representative entity which allows the mind to know material objects.

Such a third entity, however, looks very much like a third man. Malebranche could not say that ideas were material, for the role of ideas is simply to permit the mind to know mediately material objects which cannot be known directly. Material ideas themselves could not be known directly. (And if they could, why could not other material objects be known directly?) Also, if ideas were material, other mediate entities would have to be introduced to mediate knowledge of them. And so it seems for external Malebranchian ideas as well. If they are non-mental external entities, will it not be necessary to have some mediate entity for knowing them? If a bridge is needed to know external objects which are unlike the mind, has not Malebranche suggested a system in which external ideas are needed to mediate knowledge of external ideas *ad infinitum?*

It is assumed in the above paragraph that Malebranche's external ideas could help us attain knowledge of material objects. It rather appears that ideas which are neither mental nor material, and neither substance nor modification, cannot possibly represent material substances and modifications. Such ideas would be unlike both mind and matter. This is the stumbling block which Malebranche seems unable to avoid. He insists upon the epistemological likeness principle, this being his reason for denying that sensations are representative of material objects (since sensations are mental modifications), and for denying that ideas are mental modifications (since ideas are representative of material objects). Consequently, if external ideas are to represent material objects, it would seem that they must be like them in some way, but this they cannot be.

Malebranche faces these problems primarily by saying that it is the nature of ideas to represent. He remarks, as do the orthodox Cartesians, that some of the ways of God are mysterious. He recognizes that his external – third entity – ideas have no place in the Cartesian ontological framework, but rather than altering that framework, he tries to add to it by calling upon God to be the place of representative entities which have no place in a substantial God nor in an ontological structure which is still basically that of substances and their modifications.

Both Malebranche and the orthodox Cartesians adhere to the principle that direct acquaintance is necessary for knowledge. If it is impossible for the mind to be directly acquainted with material objects, then mediating representative ideas are necessary to account for our knowledge of these material objects. That it seemed obvious to these philosophers that the mind could not be directly acquainted with material objects derives from their explicit or implicit acceptance of the causal likeness principle. If the mind could be directly acquainted with material objects, mind and matter would be in immediate relation, which could only come about if they were enough alike to *engage* one another. This very engagement is disallowed because of the difference in essence between the two substances. The danger feared was not – as some later philosophers believed – that any contact between mind and matter would lead to subjectivism, but that direct acquaintance of mind with matter would imply that the mind is material. And materialism was the bastion of the blasphemist and the atheist. The strictness with which the distinction between mind and matter was kept, and the insistence that mind cannot be directly acquainted with matter, is based partially if not wholly on the horror of the likeness which would have to be admitted between mind and matter if they stood in this relationship.

Malebranche and the orthodox Cartesians also adhere explicitly or implicitly to the epistemological likeness principle, which means that the only things with which the mind can be directly acquainted are mental entities like itself. They all assert that these entities are ideas. But, what about our knowledge of God and other minds which are also mental? They, too, are known by way of representative ideas, and though there is no problem about the possibility of their being represented by ideas since they are not unlike them (except one which we shall discuss when treating Berkeley), it is puzzling why we cannot know them directly. The reason seems simple enough. *The only possible explication for direct acquaintance in the Cartesian system is that which makes it the same as the relation between a substance and its modifications.* Malebranche himself announces in the *Recherche* that he is sure that no one will disagree with him when he says that all the mind knows directly is its own ideas.[1] He can depend upon this lack of disagreement

---

[1] Malebranche, Nicolas. *De la Recherche de la vérité où l'on traite de la nature de l'esprit de l'homme, et de l'usage qu'il en doit faire pour éviter l'erreur des sciences.* In *Oeuvres complètes.* 20 volumes. Direction: André Robinet. (Paris: J. Vrin, 1958–), I, 413.

simply because it seems obvious that the mind is directly acquainted with its own properties which directly modify it. The intimate union between a substance and its modifications does service for the Cartesians in the guise of the mind being directly acquainted with its own ideas.

For Malebranche, sensations are modifications of the mind. The mind is directly acquainted with these sensations, but through this acquaintance the mind knows nothing more than the sensations themselves, for they are non-representative. Malebranche recognizes that this relation of direct acquaintance is internal to the mind; in effect, it is nothing more than the relation of a substance to its own modifications.

Malebranche's external ideas are not modifications of the mind. Consequently, when he says that the mind is directly acquainted with *external* ideas, he trades upon a notion of direct acquaintance which is no longer available to him. And he does not go on to give an explication of a new relationship of direct acquaintance, that is, one which is different from the direct acquaintance which depends upon (or is) the direct relation between a substance and its modifications. What Malebranche offers is the statement that God illuminates the ideas and thus shares them with us, allowing us to know them. Malebranche could possibly explicate *illumination* in the way the Scholastics do, with the notion of sharing. But he does not do this, since he is quite aware of the problems it would raise. Instead, he treats illumination as a form of revelation, once more calling upon God to bolster with His mysterious power an inexplicable occurrence.

Malebranche is certainly trying to solve the problem of how we know external objects by way of ideas, by breaking out of the ontological pattern of substance and modification. But he succeeds (at least within the Cartesian framework he accepts) only in making it as difficult to understand how a mind can know external ideas, as it formerly had been to explain how a mind can know external material objects. For even if we should grant Malebranche's contention that external ideas represent external objects through these ideas being God's ideas, he does not explain how *we* could be directly acquainted with them, and hence does not explain how we could know them.

There is a final problem connected with a notion of direct acquaintance which depends upon or is identical with the relation between a substance and its modifications. It raises once more the spectre of thinking matter. For if mind is directly acquainted with its own modifications because they modify it, why could not matter be directly acquainted with its modifications? There are, of course, several answers to this. Matter is not active, and it does not think. Being acquainted with something is a form of thinking. But, in giving these answers one may simply be begging the question. If direct acquaintance is grounded in the relation of a substance to its modifications, this relation is what is basic. And material things do have modifications. The only move at this point is to assert that the utter difference between mind and matter extends to the relation each has with its own modifications. The relation of a mental substance to its modifications is very different from the relation of a material substance to its modifications. The relation amounts to direct acquaintance between minds and mental modifi- cations (the Cartesians might say), but does not amount to this for material things and material modifications.

Both the orthodox Cartesians and Malebranche failed to give satisfactory answers to the problems facing Cartesianism. Their failures led to the downfall of Cartesianism, but their struggles heralded the way to the development of new metaphysics rid of the shackles of an ontology of substance and modification.

The orthodox Cartesians abandoned the likeness principles *because* they kept the Cartesian ontology. Existents, for them, can be only either substances or modifications of substances. It is evident to them that mind and matter differ in essence, and that matter is known by ideas which are modifications of mind. Hence, the principles that like can only cause and be known by like must be erroneous, for it simply *is* the case that there is causal interaction between mind and matter, and that mind knows matter without similarity. Hence, they abandon the likeness principles common to both Scholasticism and Cartesianism but offer no substitute principles to shore up Cartesian causality and epistemology other then the statement that God can make it so. We have seen that part of their inability stems from their implicit re- tention of the likeness principles.

Malebranche retains the likeness principles. He abandons causal interaction between mind and matter. His important innovation is the introduction of an entity external to the ontological pattern of sub- stance and modification common to both Scholasticism and Carte- sianism. He does this by denying that for something to be *in* the mind, it must be a modification *of* the mind. Malebranche finds it necessary to take this step to preserve knowledge by way of representative ideas, for modifications of the mind certainly cannot resemble and thus cannot represent material things. He still believes, however, that direct acquaintance is necessary for knowledge. Since he cannot attain this by appealing to the relation of a substance to its own modifications, he speaks of God allowing us to know external ideas through the mystery of illumination. Further, having broken with the Cartesian ontological framework, he offers no explanation of what might be a new ontological structure. Instead, he does as the orthodox Cartesians do, he avers again to the mysterious ways of God. It is to his credit that he has seen that ideas external to (in the sense of not being modifications of) all minds are necessary to begin to solve the epistemological problems facing Cartesianism. But just as the orthodox Cartesians offer no new principles to take the place of the likeness principles which they find must be abandoned, so neither does Malebranche offer any new ontological explanations to establish a place for his new entity, the external idea.

Both the orthodox Cartesians and Malebranche are bound to the principles they supposedly abandon. They show this by resorting to God to repair their systems. The orthodox Cartesians can find it mysterious how mind can know matter, which is different from mind, only *by reference to* the likeness principles they purport to abandon. And Malebranche can find the real ontological status of ideas inexplicable only *with reference to* the ontology of substance and modification with which he seems to be breaking.

# CHAPTER VII

# POST-CARTESIAN DEVELOPMENTS
# OF THE WAY OF IDEAS

A monistic solution to the Cartesian problems is suggested in Descartes' own writings. Concerning the interaction between substances, they are alike for Descartes as substances created by God. And though he stresses that mind *is* thinking and matter *is* extension, he does not always compress (or confuse) substance with its essence. This could be construed as a denial of absolute dualism. Hence, interaction could take place because of real ontological likeness between the two substances. This likeness might also serve to explain how ideas represent material things, except for the claim that sensations are not representative. Sensations would have just as much likeness to material things as would ideas, so the representative character of ideas cannot be this likeness alone if sensations are to be non-representative. There is a possibility that Descartes could solve the epistemological problem by denying the epistemological likeness principle. He does sometimes say that ideas and sensations are innate. If they arise only upon the *occasion* of real interaction between mind and matter, there is no need to say that their representative character is *caused* by this interaction. Innate ideas could a priori (from God) have a representative character, while sensations do not. One could not object that they must both represent because both are caused by interaction, for the representative character would *not* be caused by interaction. To this solution one might object that there is no clear notion of what this representative character might be, while the fact that there is likeness between sensations (as well as ideas) and material objects is enough to establish that sensations (as well as ideas) can represent material objects.

If Spinoza's system is a development of the implications of Cartesianism (and many thought it was), then he can be seen as solving Cartesian problems by denying the ontological dualism. Mind and matter become nothing more than parallel modifications of one substance, God. Spinoza also denies interactionism. He could probably incorporate most of the other principles, even interactionism, though it may be that his definitions would alter their sense too radically for one to say that he was keeping them as the Cartesian principles indicated above.

Foucher thought the solution lay in finding an essential similarity between mind and matter. He accepted the Cartesian compression of essence and substance, so did not see the possibility for this similarity in Cartesianism. Rather, he was much intrigued by Leibniz's notion that force is the essence of substance. In a correspondence with Leibniz which extended over 20 years (see Chapter VIII), Foucher suggested that if force is the essence of substance, then one might explain therewith the interaction which obviously takes place between mind and matter. He thought there could be a possibility of interaction in a plurality of substances only if they were all essentially the same. Leibniz, however, explains why it *seems* that interaction takes place, rather than explaining how it is that it *does* take place, even though he suggests denying the ontological dualism.

Locke also admits the possibility of denying the dualism. He says that extension is only a modification of matter, and thinking only a modification of mind; we do not know the essence of either substance. Consequently, it is possible that the two substances are like one another even enough to support similar modifications. Locke also claims that ideas do resemble, and thus represent, material modifications; this seems to be evidence that mental substance also resembles material substance. Of course, in such case, the problem of why sensations are non-representative would still remain.

Monistic solutions were almost universally rejected by Cartesians and their opponents alike. There are a number of reasons for this, and it is well to consider them, for the dualism is the seat of the difficulties which infect Cartesian metaphysics. First, they all undoubtedly thought dualism was an empirical fact. Second, without dualism, a system could hardly be called Cartesian. Descartes had established it, and it certainly is important to most of his disciples that they carry the spirit if not the letter of the master. Third, less likely, but possible, Cartesians may have thought that in the face of problems, adjustments elsewhere in the system would lead to a more elegant system than the rejection of dualism would provide. Fourth, however, there is finally a historical reason which was perhaps sufficient for all. Spinoza developed a monism and was for it called an atheist. Whoever developed a monism was in danger of being accused of saying that God is material. Hence, though Foucher suggested a possibly monistic way out, he did not develop it. And Locke, arguing much as had Foucher, throws doubt upon the clear-cut distinction between matter and mind. For saying that we do not know the essences of mind and matter, and thus opening the possibility that they are similar enough for material and mental modifications to be properties of either mind or matter – if matter could be modified by ideas, then matter could think –, Locke, also, was accused of being an atheist. It does not seem strictly necessary in reading Descartes to deny all similarity between mind and matter, but as a matter of fact it was prudent to keep this distinction if possible.

Despite the failure of Cartesianism as a metaphysical system, Cartesian principles guided post-Cartesian development. John Locke, for example, keeps a dualism of mind and matter, an ontology of substance and modification, and both likeness principles. He even incorporates into his system a variety of Scholastic elements, specifically, occult forces. His system can be seen as an attempt to make the Cartesian way of ideas intelligible – he read the Cartesians, probably including the debate between Malebranche and Foucher –, [1] and in this sense the failure of his system can be seen as sharing that of the Cartesian way of ideas.

For Locke, an idea is "whatsoever is the object of the understanding when a man thinks"; it is "whatever is meant by phantasm, notion, species, or whatever it is which the mind can be employed about in thinking." [2] Ideas of material objects are of two sorts: some resemble (or are images of) the qualities of bodies, and others do (or are) not. This distinction is coextensive with the Cartesian distinction between ideas and sensations.

Bodies actually have the primary qualities of solidity, extension, figure, motion or rest, and number; these qualities have the power to cause ideas which resemble (and hence represent) them. Certain combinations of primary qualities are called secondary qualities, and they have the power to cause sensations which do not resemble (and

---

[1] Lough, John, "Locke's Reading during his Stay in France," *The Library, A Quarterly Review of Bibliography, Transactions of the Bibliographical Society*, Third Series, VIII (1953), 229–258. Among the books Lough lists Locke as owning are the following: Malebranche's *Recherche* (247, 254), Desgabets' *Critique de la Critique* (248, 253, 256), Foucher's *Critique de la Recherche* (246, 257), and Foucher's *Réponse pour la Critique* (257).

[2] Locke, John, *An Essay Concerning Human Understanding*, edited by A. C. Fraser, 2 volumes (Oxford: Clarendon Press, 1894), I, I, 8.(Since there is no standard edition of the *Essay*, references are made only to Book, Chapter, and Paragraph.)

hence do not represent) anything in material objects. Sensible qualities in bodies, therefore, are nothing but powers to cause us to have sensations. Primary qualities are seen to belong to bodies because of their permanence; whatever alteration one can effect upon a body, it still will have the primary qualities.[1] That we mistakenly attribute colors, for example, to material objects is due to the weakness of our senses; powerful microscopes, Locke contends, would undoubtedly show us that the minute particles from which all things are made have only the primary qualities.[2]

As in the Cartesian way, all we know immediately are ideas.

Since the mind, in all its thoughts and reasonings, hath no other immediate object but its own ideas, which it alone does or can contemplate, it is evident that our knowledge is only conversant about them.[3]

Thus, all our knowledge of external things is mediated by ideas.[4] About external things we know that their modifications must be supported by a substance. Our ideas are known to be modifications of spiritual substance; primary qualities and powers are known to be modifications of material substance. However, unlike the Cartesians, Locke says that the essences of the two substances are unknown. Extension is merely a modification of matter; thinking is merely a modification of mind.[5] Each of these substances is "but a supposed I-know-not-what, to support those ideas we call 'accidents'." [6]

Sensations do not represent any real qualities in material things, but they have a reality "in that steady correspondence they have with the distinct constitutions of real beings." Locke goes on to state clearly the correspondence between things and sensations which the Cartesians assume when they say that the role of sensations is to guide us in our everyday contacts with other bodies:

Our simple ideas are all real, all agree to the reality of things. Not that they are all of them the images or representations of what does exist; the contrary whereof, in all but [ideas of] the primary qualities of bodies, hath been already showed. But though whiteness and coldness are no more in snow than pain is; yet these ideas [sensations] of whiteness and coldness, pain, &c., being in us the effects of powers in things without us, ordained by our

---

[1] *Ibid.*, II, VIII, 9–10.
[2] *Ibid.*, II, XXIII, 11.
[3] *Ibid.*, IV, I, 1.
[4] *Ibid.*, IV, IV, 3.
[5] *Ibid.*, II, XIII, 19.
[6] *Ibid.*, II, XXIII, 15.

Maker to produce in us such sensations, they are real ideas in us, whereby we distinguish the qualities that are really in things themselves.[1]

It is significant that Locke states that this non-resembling correspondence is not a case of representation.

Locke, as does Leibniz, recognizes that Cartesian mechanistic explanations of perception are not enough to explain how material objects cause ideas and sensations. Cartesian physics does not even explain how material objects can cause changes in one another. So Locke introduces a third power which combinations of primary qualities have, a power to rearrange the primary qualities of other bodies. The result of this alteration is that the changed bodies then have (because of the rearrangement of their primary qualities) different powers of causing sensations and ideas than they formally had. Besides primary qualities, then, bodies have three sorts of powers: the power to cause ideas which resemble primary qualities, the power to cause sensations which correspond to but do not resemble combinations of primary qualities, and the power to rearrange primary qualities in other bodies.[2] These powers are obviously Scholastic occult forces. A Cartesian might very well say that they explain nothing. The power one body has to alter another is simply a Scholastic way of describing what takes place according to the laws of impact, something which is perfectly understandable in itself. The postulation of powers to cause sensations and ideas is nothing more than an unilluminating way (Cartesians might say) of admitting that though we can describe with a physics of impact what takes place in the material world during perception, we do not know the mysterious ways of God Who makes it so that these impacts cause sensations and ideas.

Locke's system raises numerous problems. Do we have ideas of powers? A Cartesian would say that we do not because we cannot, powers being nothing in material things that we actually know. If there really are powers, Locke carelessly confuses them with the actual primary qualities or modifications. At best, according to his system, we can infer their existence; but this may be no more than adhering to the principle that all things – including ideas and sensations – must have a cause. Must one necessarily infer that since ideas represent, and sensations correspond to (if they do) material objects, that these material objects have the power to cause sensations and ideas? Malebranche, at least, infers from the fact that sensations and ideas are

[1] *Ibid.*, II, XXX, 2.
[2] *Ibid.*, II, VIII, 23–24.

totally unlike material objects, that they obviously cannot be caused by material objects. As for ideas which resemble and hence represent primary qualities, ontologically both ideas and sensations are modifications of the mind. It is difficult to understand how something unextended could be an image of something extended. Such criticisms of Locke's way of ideas, similar to Foucher's criticisms of the Cartesian way, were actually made by Lee and Sergeant.[1]

It might be thought that with his recognition of the correspondence of sensations to material things, Locke presents a possible new sense of representation which was open to, but curiously ignored by, the orthodox Cartesians. For whatever reason the Cartesians ignored it, it still remains that sensations are nothing more than signs of material objects. As such, we have seen, they cannot be expected to give knowledge – to represent – material objects unless these material objects are known previously in some other way.

Locke obviously agrees that an idea must resemble its object in order to represent it. He also holds to the Cartesian dictum that direct acquaintance is necessary between knower and known, and, like the Cartesians, makes this relation coextensive with that of substance to modification. Consequently, he is necessarily bound to knowledge only of ideas. He remarks, as does Leibniz, that if there are any external triangles, then they have the properties known in contemplating the idea of a triangle.[2] But he would have to admit that one can never really be certain that our ideas are truly of their external objects if this can be ascertained only by comparing the object with the idea. Ultimately, Locke appeals to God, as do the orthodox Cartesians. God has ordained that our ideas represent external things (or at least their primary qualities) as they are in themselves. And there is a final admonition: Stop yearning for deeper knowledge, for God has given us faculties adequate to the attainment of as much knowledge as our state requires.[3]

Putting aside other difficulties, could Locke's ideas resemble and hence represent primary qualities of material things? It seems possible, for Locke admits that he does not know the essence of mind and matter. If these two substances have similar essences, then resemblance between their modifications could be supported. Locke reports what seems to take place, which is that ideas do resemble material modifications;

---

[1] See: Yolton, John W., *John Locke and the Way of Ideas* (Oxford: Oxford University Press, 1956).
[2] Locke. *Essay*, IV, IV, 6.
[3] *Ibid.*, IV, IV, 4.

consequently, one might very well infer that mind and matter are similar substances. We have already seen that the monistic solution was not a popular one.

Whether Locke was trying to repair the Cartesian system or simply to state the truth as he saw it, he lay himself open to attack from all sides. The Cartesians attacked him for introducing occult qualities; the sceptics attacked his notion of representative ideas; and the bigots attacked him for opening the doors to materialism and atheism. Locke leads the Cartesian way of ideas to disaster. The reason for this probably lies in his incomplete digestion of continental metaphysics.

George Berkeley's philosophy of ideas also can be viewed as an attempt to circumvent the problems inherent in Cartesianism. Berkeley's studies and earliest publications were contemporaneous with the last major publications of Cartesianism,[1] and there is little doubt that he knew of the problems inherent in Cartesianism and of Malebranche's solutions to them. He was specifically concerned to deprive the sceptics of the foothold they had in the theory of representative ideas.[2] Whether or not Berkeley developed his philosophy of ideas in an attempt to circumvent the problems inherent in Cartesianism, it is illuminating to consider it as though he had. A consideration of his system in the context of Cartesianism throws new light upon the epistemological roles and ontological status of Berkeley's ideas and notions.

What will become apparent is the following: Cartesian problems arise primarily through difficulties of characterizing the relationships between two substances which differ in essence. Berkeley, in denying that matter exists, abandons the Cartesian principles having to do with the ontological dualism (see Chapter III and Appendix I). He thus, in one stroke, dispenses with the problems given rise to by the first and second of Foucher's criticisms outlined in Chapter III and Appendix II. There are no problems concerning how two substances which differ in essence can causally interact, nor concerning how one can know the other, for there is only one kind of substance. Berkeley, however, evades the problems concerning the relationships of one substance to another different one, only to find problems concerning the relation between a substance and its modifications.

---

[1] Antoine Le Grand's *An Entire Body of Philosophy, According to the Principles of the Famous Renate des Cartes* (London: Samuel Roycroft was published in 1694. Malebranche's last *Éclaircissement* to the *Recherche* was published in 1712. For the influence of Bayle and Malebranche on Berkeley see Luce, A. A.: *Berkeley and Malebranche, A Study in the Origins of Berkeley's Thought* (London: Oxford University Press, 1934).

[2] On Berkeley's relation to scepticism, see: Popkin, Richard H. "Berkeley and Pyrrhonism," *Review of Metaphysics*, V, 1951–52, 223–246.

With reference to Cartesianism, Berkeley's position can be reached as follows: He utilizes Foucher's third and fourth criticisms against the Cartesian distinction between sensations and ideas to show that we cannot know material things.[1] He agrees with the principle that direct acquaintance is necessary for knowledge, and then goes on to say that what we know is all that exists. Since we cannot know matter, it cannot exist. He thus denies ontological dualism and interactionism. Sensations and ideas are not ontologically different from one another, and neither of them is representative of things; sensations and ideas *are* things. By doing away with external matter and the representative ideas by way of which it is supposedly known, Berkeley undercuts much sceptical argument. We can be certain of our knowledge of ideas, because we are directly acquainted with them and they are all – save minds and relations – there is to know.

Berkeley shows his adherence to the causal and epistemological likeness principles in two ways. First, he uses them in his attack upon matter and the theory of representative ideas. One of his principles is: "*Nothing can give to another that which it hath not itself.*" [2] From this he reasons that where there is no likeness between two substances, there can be no causal interaction. Since the two Cartesian substances are utterly different, it is impossible for matter to cause ideas. He points out that since matter is inactive, it is contradictory even to say that there is interaction between bodies; but even if there were some sort of material action, if matter is said to be inactive to distinguish it as contrary to mind which is active, then even a special kind of material action would not permit matter to interact with mind. It is quite inconceivable, Berkeley says, that an unthinking thing could produce thought.[3]

Second, when considering the possibility that ideas might represent external objects, Berkeley insists that nothing can be like an idea but an idea.[4] From this he concludes that the only things ideas could represent are other ideas, because they resemble one another in being ideas. Representation is not the primary function of ideas, of course; it is only accidental upon their likeness to one another. Thus it would be wrong to characterize Berkeley as Malebranche without matter.

---

[1] Berkeley, George, *Three Dialogues between Hylas and Philonous* in *The Works of George Berkeley, Bishop of Cloyne*. Edited by A. A. Luce and T. E. Jessop (London: Thomas Nelson and Sons, Ltd., 1948–1957), II, 171ff; *A Treatise Concerning the Principles of Human Knowledge*, Principles 8–15, *ibid.*, 44–77.

[2] Berkeley, George, *Three Dialogues*, 236.

[3] *Ibid.*, 242–243, 257–258, 216.

[4] *Ibid.*, 206; *Principles*, 44.

For then he would have representative ideas which have no material world to represent, and which are different from sensations.

Berkeley was also bound to the all-inclusive ontological type-distinction between substance and modification. He adhered to this pattern particularly in saying that ideas depend upon minds in that their being is being perceived by a mind.[1] *Ideas, for Berkeley, must be mental modifications.*

There are four direct arguments for establishing this claim: First, and least impressive, for Locke and the Cartesians what is perceived by the mind are ideas, and for them ideas are modifications of the mind.

Second, Berkeley denies the ontological dualism, and in denying that anything is material he seems to be asserting that everything is mental. Of course he need not maintain that mental substances and mental modifications are all there is, but in ordinary ontological parlance this is all that would remain. If extension, for example, is not a modification of matter, but only an idea of extension, it seems plausible to suppose that as an idea it still has the characteristic of being a modification; minds, for Berkeley, are the only things of which it could be a modification.

Third, he uses Foucher's arguments for establishing that if sensations are in the mind, then so are ideas. Many philosophers thought sensations were modifications of the mind. If it is correct to say that Berkeley modeled his ideas on Malebranchian ideas (as has often been suggested),[2] it is also the case that Berkeley compounded these Malebranchian ideas with sensations, and Malebranchian sensations are modifications of the mind. Berkeley is seldom interpreted as elevating sensations to ideas; he is usually interpreted as reducing ideas to sensations.[3]

[1] This dependence need not necessarily mean that the dependent item is a property or modification. Spinoza seemed to believe it did. Certainly one of the problems in insisting upon a substance's dependence upon God was that this might mean the substance was a modification of God. Substances can be said to be causally dependent upon God, but even here there is a tradition of supposing that God's causal activity is merely the flowering out of His potentialities. Leibniz, for example, conceives a monad as having the power to cause and support as effects its own modifications. In this sense, the distinction between causal dependence and dependence in the sense of being a modification is but nominal. For a Spinozistic treatment of Descartes, see a doctoral dissertation completed at the University of Michigan by Vernon, Thomas S. *The Metaphysical Role of Ideas in the Philosophy of Descartes.* (Ann Arbor: University Microfilms, 1963).

[2] For example, in Luce *op. cit.*, and in Popkin, Richard H. "The New Realism of Bishop Berkeley" in *George Berkeley*, University of California Publications in Philosophy, XXIX (Berkeley and Los Angeles: University of California Press, 1957), 1–19.

[3] See also Fritz, Anita D., "Berkeley's Self – Its Origin in Malebranche," *Journal of the History of Ideas*, XV, 1954, 554–572; Bracken, Harry M. "Berkeley and Mental Acts," *Theoria*, XXVI, 1960, 140–146; Bracken, Harry M. "Berkeley and Malebranche on Ideas," *The Modern Schoolman*,XLI, 1963, 1–15; and Guéroult, Martial, *Berkeley* (Paris: Aubier, 1956).

Fourth, and most important, if Berkeley keeps the ontological type-distinction between substance and modification, then by posing ideas as mental modifications he has a ready and familiar ground for the relation of direct acquaintance of a mind with an idea. His lack of concern for how a mind can be directly acquainted with ideas can be explained by the fact that it is for him dependent on, or coextensive with, or the same as the familiar relation of dependence between a substance and its modifications.

However, in Principle 49 Berkeley contrasts being "in the mind" ... "by way of *mode* or *attribute*" with being in the mind "by way of idea." [1] If it is to be claimed that for him ideas *are* mental modifications, the claim can be established only by showing that he reasons as though they are, whatever he says to the contrary. There are five lines of evidence that Berkeley depends upon the relation between substance and modification in reasoning about ideas. First, Berkeley creates problems by denying that God has ideas of pain.[2] If the question were, "Is God modified by pain?", then Berkeley's denial is perfectly understandable. Since Berkeley's example is the idea of pain, and he equates having a pain with knowing (perceiving) a pain, this shows that he reasons about ideas as though they were modifications of the mind. If the dependence ideas have upon being perceived were a *mere* causal dependence, then why not allow God to cause-perceive-know them? But if the dependence is that of modification upon substance, if the knowing relation is to be explicated with reference to the relation of substance to modification, then it *does* pose a problem to assert that God knows pain. This would mean that He is modified by pain.

Second, since ideas and minds are both mental, it would seem easy enough to assert that ideas resemble and thus can represent minds. But Berkeley explicitly denies this, and in doing so he understands something which was clear to Descartes, though somewhat unclear to Malebranche. In answering objections raised by Gassendi Descartes says, "there is more difference between ... accidents and a substance, than there is between two substances." [3] Berkeley recognizes this in saying that ideas are passive, whereas minds are active.[4] Minds can cause ideas since they are both mental, but since ideas are

[1] Berkeley, *Principles*, 61–62.
[2] Berkeley, *Three Dialogues*, 240–241.
[3] Descartes, René, "Letter from M. Descartes to M. Clerselier to Serve as a Reply to a Selection of the Principle Objections taken by M. Gassendi to the Preceding Replies," *Works* translated by E. S. Haldane and G. R. T. Ross (New York: Dover, 1955), II, 132.
[4] Berkeley, *Three Dialogues*, 231ff.

passive they cannot represent active minds even if the ideas are mental like minds. This would pertain whether or not ideas are mental modifications. Even mental ideas which are not mental modifications could not represent minds if these ideas are passive. However, it seems reasonable to suppose that ideas are considered here by Berkeley as mental modifications. Their passiveness would be a reflection of their dependence upon the substance they modify, and their inability to represent minds would rest on the basic ontological difference between substance and modification.[1]

Third, relations are known only through notions. Certainly no idea which is itself a modification of the mind could resemble as such a relation between two entities. The very being of a mode resides in its dependence upon a substance. So if Berkeley thought of ideas as related to the mind as modifications are to a substance, he would certainly find them inadequate (as he did) for representing relations.

Fourth, Berkeley says that we know our own mind because we are directly acquainted with its ideas (recall that modifications are often said to be nothing more than a substance modified); but that we know other minds through notions.[2] Could these notions be modifications of the mind? If they were active modifications, then they could indeed represent active minds by being like them. Other minds could act upon our minds to cause them, so the causal likeness principle would be satisfied as well. But Berkeley is concerned to deny representationalism in order to escape scepticism; if he introduces representative notions he will open himself to sceptical attack, whether they are mental modifications or not. Suppose, then, that one interpreted notions as mere occasions (mental modifications or not) for direct acquaintance with other minds. If this were so, then this direct acquaintance would be of a different sort than that pertaining between substantial minds and ideas which are mental modifications. For other minds certainly are not, for Berkeley, modifications of one's own mind. But Berkeley is no occasionalist. By ridding himself of matter, he allows for causal interaction between the substances which remain; causal interaction between minds – at least between God's and others – is possible because of their likeness one to another. In any case, Berkeley says that notions

---

[1] Could an active mind have a passive modification? It must be argued here that a passive idea is not inert in the sense that Cartesian matter is. As a modification of an active substance, an idea would have to be active as opposed to inertness, but it could be passive in the sense that the shape if a moving ship is in motion, but does not activate the motion. The passiveness of an idea would be that its being – or activity – is provided by the mind.

[2] *Ibid.*, 232.

are necessary for the mediate knowledge of other minds. It is clear why we cannot know other minds directly, if we can be directly acquainted only with our own modifications: What other reason is there for restricting direct acquaintance to ideas, than the assumption that being directly acquainted with something makes it a part – a modification – of one's self?

Fifth, Berkeley has trouble with his doctrine of notions – how we are directly acquainted with them and how they make things with which we are not directly acquainted known – *because* he does *not* reason about them as though they were modifications of the mind. Berkeley's notions, modeled on Malebranchian ideas which are external to the mind in the sense of not being modifications of it, are entities outside the ontological framework of substance and modification. For someone bound to reasoning within this framework, as Berkeley was, such external entities are not only ontologically unclassifiable, their role cannot help but be obscure. Berkeley has difficulty with his doctrine of notions because he has no ready explication of how one could be directly acquainted with something external to the mind. He could not depend upon the familiar relation between substance and modification in clarifying the role of notions.

But Berkeley and many of his readers find the mind's knowledge of ideas unproblematic. This is because he conceives of the *having* or perceiving of an idea, or of an idea's being *in* the mind, as though the idea were a property of the mind; consequently, he can depend upon the Cartesian relation of dependence between a modification and a substance to establish direct acquaintance of a mind with its ideas. The fact that he did not feel an explanation was necessary for how the mind is directly acquainted with ideas is evidence that even though Berkeley explicitly denies that ideas are modifications of the mind, he reasons about them as though they were.

Berkeley, like Malebranche, can be seen as striving to break out of the Cartesian ontological pattern of substance and modification. Neither of these philosophers could make this break successfully because they were still dependent upon the explanatory force of the relation between substance and modification. The dependence indicated in the principle that *perceiving* is the essence of mind, and *being perceived* is the essence of ideas appears in Berkeley's philosophy as the dependence of a modification upon the substance it modifies. Berkeley could not perceive other minds because their essence is not being perceived – they are not modifications of the perceiver's mind.

But he was certain that we do know other minds, so he introduced notions which are *in* the mind or *had* by the mind without being modifications of the mind. But how can we be directly acquainted with them? And even if we can be, if they are representative of minds, they must be like minds. And if we can be directly acquainted with something like minds, why not with minds themselves? Finally, if they are representative of minds (whether or not they resemble them), all the sceptical paradoxes left at the heels of Locke and the Cartesians would come to hound Berkeley.

Berkeley escaped the problems of causal and epistemological relations between two different substances, but he could not escape the problems inherent in a dependence upon the relation between substance and modification. He strove to break out of this pattern, but he could not do so. If Berkeley had taken ideas as external to – in the sense of not being modifications of – the mind, he could not have taken it for granted that we are directly acquainted with ideas, but would have had to explicate a sense of direct acquaintance which makes it different from a relation which is dependent upon or coextensive with if not identical to the relation of a substance to its modifications. That Berkeley was unable to give such an explication is evident in his treatment of notions, external entities whose epistemic role and ontological status remain problematic in Berkeley's system.

However, Berkeley, following the lead of Malebranche, did continue the break with Cartesian ontology. Notions, like Malebranchian ideas, have no place in an all-inclusive ontology of substance and modification. But he failed to make the break clean-cut, and it remained for Hume to dispense completely with the pattern of substance and modification,[1] just as Berkeley dispenses with the ontological dualism of different substances.

In a Cartesian context, then, Berkeley's ideas are knowable because the mind is directly acquainted with its own modifications; his notions are problematic because they represent an attempt to escape the ontological pattern of substance and modification.

There is a question we have not yet asked in this study which can appropriately be raised here. Can the question, "What is an idea?", be construed as an ontological question at all? Obviously ideas do have ontological status for all the philosophers considered so far. Some of them indicate aspects other than the ontological, but the burden of this

---

[1] Hume, David, *A Treatise of Human Nature.* Edited by L. A. Selby-Bigge (Oxford: Clarendon Press, 1955), 232ff.

study has been to show that the ontological status of ideas is crucial in determining their epistemic efficacy, for example, when a philosopher believes that likeness is necessary between an idea and what it represents. Attempts to escape the weight of ontological status for ideas have been characterized as attempts to break out of the ontological pattern of substance and modification. Everything is either a substance or a modification. So long as this principle is held, the way of ideas is doomed. One could say ideas are nothing, or at least not entities, or one could try to introduce a new ontological entity. But as Malebranche and Berkeley illustrate, it is difficult to characterize such an entity. There is another alternative. Everything might be of the same ontological status. Then if likeness is necessary for representation, everything could represent everything, for anything that is would be an idea; ideas are like ideas. David Hume might be seen as taking this expedient. We shall introduce him now near the close of this study, however, not as one who reduced ontological categories to one, but as one who broke entirely with the ontological structure of substance and modification.

David Hume,[1] like Berkeley, came to sceptical conclusions about Cartesian ontology after reading Bayle and Locke. Not only does he deny the ontological dualism, but he also explicitly denies the all-inclusive ontological type-distinction between substance and modification.[2] Foucher argues that Cartesians do not know the essence of mind and matter as they claim to, Malebranche that we have an idea of the essence of matter but not of mind, Locke that we cannot know the essence of either, and Berkeley that we have a notion of the essence of mind but not of matter. Hume concludes that we have no idea, and thus no knowledge, of any substance at all.

Perceptions, i.e., what is immediately perceived, are divided by Hume into impressions and ideas. Impressions have more force and vivacity than the ideas which are derived from them; every idea is

---

[1] On Hume's relation to scepticism, see four recent articles by Richard H. Popkin: "David Hume: His Pyrrhonism and his Critique of Pyrrhonism" *Philosophical Quarterly*, I (1950–1951), 385–407; "David Hume and the Pyrrhonian Controversy" *Review of Metaphysics*, VI (1952–1953), 65–81; "The Sceptical Crisis and the Rise of Modern Philosophy, III" *Review of Metaphysics*, VII (1953–1954), 499–510; and "The Sceptical Precursors of David Hume" *Philosophy and Phenomenological Research*, XVI, 1955, 61–71. For a different viewpoint and the best overall commentary on Hume's philosophy, see: Smith, Norman Kemp, *The Philosophy of David Hume, A Critical Study of its Origins and Central Doctrines* (London: Macmillan, 1941).

[2] Hume, David, *op. cit.*, 232ff. Hume is not entirely original in the issues with which we are concerned here, sometimes following Bayle, as Kemp Smith remarks, "with almost verbal consistency." For an introduction to Bayle's influence on Hume, see: Smith, Norman Kemp, *op. cit.*, 325–338.

preceded by an impression. Perceptions include everything Locke calls ideas, and are the only objects we know. From this Berkeleian conclusion that the only objects which we can immediately *know* to exist are impressions and ideas, Hume argues that impressions and ideas are the only objects which *do* exist. When we examine our idea of substance, for example, we find that it is not an idea of an independently existing entity at all, but only a compound idea of a collection of related perceptions. Our ideas of modes are similarly found not to be of dependent entities, but of other collections of related ideas. No impression or idea in itself carries with it the notion that it is dependent as a modification upon some substance.[1] Such substances, however, would resemble traditional mind and matter very little. Like Berkeley, Hume dismisses Locke's notion of "material" substance as an I-know-not-what.[2] Hume, however, goes on to dismiss also the notion of "spiritual" substance of which we also have no idea. Selves, like material objects, are nothing more than bundles of perceptions.[3]

Hume argues as does Foucher that the primary qualities are quite as sensible as the secondary. Thus, while he admits the usefulness of the distinction, he claims no superior reality for primary over secondary qualities. In fact, Hume insists that the Cartesian implication that secondary qualities are less real than primary leads to "the most extravagant scepticism" about our knowledge of external things. Equally insidious is the notion that ideas are mediate entities in the process of knowing. Ideas, says Hume, do not make things other than themselves known. Even if they did, there would be no way to compare them with their so-called objects to check their accuracy.[4]

Hume retains the notion that representation is the same as or dependent upon resemblance. Ideas can represent impressions because they resemble them.[5] One of his reasons for concluding that we have no idea of substance is that no perception can resemble a substance. Resemblance is so basic in Hume's system that he takes it as a general rule that "no relation of any kind can subsist without some degree of resem-

---

[1] *Ibid.*, 1–17.
[2] *Ibid.*, 233.
[3] *Ibid.*, 252.
[4] *Ibid.*, 128–131, 189, 192, 228.
    Hume also has problems concerning the comparison of an idea with the impression of which it is a copy. If they are had at the same time, perhaps the greater vivacity of the impression will make it impossible to distinguish the weaker idea. If they occur at separate times, they cannot be immediately compared.
[5] *Ibid.*, 3.

blance."[1] All ideas are derived from and resemble impressions; therefore,

> as every idea is deriv'd from a preceding perception, 'tis impossible our idea of a perception, and that of an object or external existence can ever represent what are specifically different from each other.[2]

Such representation is impossible, since in Hume's terms our idea "of an object or external existence" is nothing more than a complex idea of a collection of perceptions.[3]

Hume can be seen as making sense of the Cartesian way of ideas by retaining the epistemological likeness principle, but he would be doing so only by abandoning the dualistic system which gives rise to the difficulties. Impressions are not external objects, nor do collections of them comprise external objects, but they are not internal either; they are all – together with ideas which are in essence only weaker perceptions – that exist. There is no problem of the causal interaction of substances for there are no substances. There is no essential difficulty about representation, for all existences are of the same sort. Perceptions do not in themselves point beyond to anything they must inhere in or which must cause them; they are what they are, and we can know of nothing – nothing exists – which transcends them. All the philosophers we have considered so far, even, emphatically, Foucher, were searching for knowledge of the essences of substances. With Hume the search for knowledge of qualities, powers, forms, forces, and essences or natures of substances founders at last. This is because nothing remains to which these terms might be applied; all that exists, for Hume, are impressions and ideas which are perceived to be openly what they are and nothing more.

In the role of critic of the Cartesian metaphysical system, Hume agrees with Foucher that ideas and sensations are of the same kind, and that the relation of representation is or depends upon resemblance. But instead of finding new and certain knowledge of the essences of substances as Foucher hoped someone would, Hume instead denies the possibility of the knowledge and even the existence of substances at all. And if the abandonment of the ontological pattern of substance and modification requires new explanatory support for the relations of an idea's being in the mind, and of a mind's being directly acquainted with an idea – since these relations can no longer depend upon the relation between a substance and its own modifications –, Hume can

---

[1] *Ibid.*, 15.
[2] *Ibid.*, 241.
[3] *Ibid.*, 16.

be seen as offering for this explanatory role the relation of an idea to the collection of perceptions of which it is a member.

Hume thus completes the breakdown of Cartesian metaphysics. [1] He abandons the traditional all-inclusive ontological distinction between substance and modification which Descartes inherited from the Scholastics. In destroying the ontological structure which gives rise to Cartesian problems, however, he at the same time destroys the ground for the Cartesian explanation of the relation of a mind to its own ideas. If an idea is not a modification of a substantial mind, then what is it? The contemporary concern with the ontological status of such items as concepts and propositions, and of particulars and universals, is in part a legacy from reactions to sceptical criticisms of Cartesianism in the late 17th century.

---

[1] While Hume might have been happy with the destructive role I have attributed to him, he was not satisfied with his own explanations of mind and the relations between ideas and impressions. Cf. Hume, *op. cit.*, 633–636.

# CHAPTER VIII

# LEIBNIZ AND FOUCHER

Leibniz also considered the problems of Cartesian dualism. His New System was partially inspired by Foucher's objections to Cartesianism, and can be seen as providing a way to avoid Cartesian difficulties. Hence, we shall now present an interpretation of Leibniz's New System, with emphasis on his concern with first principles, certain knowledge, and the external world. This will be done in the context of Foucher's criticisms of Leibniz. The chapter concludes with an examination of Leibniz's system in its role of solving Cartesian problems.

The correspondence between Leibniz and Foucher extends from 1676, the year Leibniz left Paris, to 1696, the year of Foucher's death.[1] Foucher sent Leibniz his works as they appeared (always with complaints about how hard it was to publish) which Leibniz read and commented upon. He valued Foucher's criticisms and sought them from him concerning his New System of philosophy. Extracts from the correspondence appeared in the *Journal des sçavans* from 1692 to 1696 [2] in which Leibniz first places his New System before the public and Foucher gives it its first critique to appear in print. Relations between the two men were most cordial throughout the twenty years.

In his *Nouveaux essais sur l'entendement humain* Leibniz remarks that he had discussed the existence of external things at length with Foucher.

Or je luy fis connoistre que la verité des choses sensibles ne consistoit que dans la liaison des phenomenes, qui devoit avoir sa raison et que c'est ce qui les distingue des songes: mais que la verité de nostre existence et de la cause des phenomenes est d'une autre nature, parce qu'elle etablit des Substances, et que les Sceptiques gastoient ce qu'ils disent de bon, en le portant trop loin,

---

[1] "Briefwechsel zwischen Leibniz und Foucher" in: *Die Philosophischen Schriften von Gottfried Wilhelm Leibniz*, Herausgegeben von C. J. Gerhardt, (Berlin: Weidmaunsche, 1875), I, 363–427.

[2] See Chapter II, p. 15, n. 4.

et en voulant même etendre leur doutes jusqu'aux experiences immediates, et jusques aux verités geometriques, ce que Mr. Foucher pourtant ne faisoit pas, et aux autres verités de raison, ce qu'il faisait un peau trop.[1]

This remark seems to apply primarily to Leibniz's first letter to Foucher of 1676. Leibniz begins:

Je demeure d'accord avec vous qu'il est de consequence que nous examinions une bonne fois toutes nos suppositions, à fin d'etablir quelque chose de solide. Car je tiens que c'est alors qu'on entend parfaitement la chose dont il s'agit, quand on peut prouver tout ce qu'on avance.[2]

Leibniz takes Foucher to be concerned with discovering truths which will assure us that there is an external world. Foucher grants the "veritez hypothetiques" which do not assure us about anything external, but only about what would be the case if there were something external similar to what the truths are about. Hence, there is no disagreement betweeen the two men about the internal truths of arithmetic, geometry, and many propositions of metaphysics, physics, and morals, "dont l'expression commode depend de definitions arbitraires choises, et dont la verité depend des axiomes que j'ay coustume d'appeler identiques." [3] Leibniz says he believes that all such hypothetical propositions should be entirely demonstrated and resolved to identities. He recognizes that this still does not give us truth about external things, so he proceeds to offer two proofs of the existence of something external. The very possibility, impossibility, or necessity of hypothetical propositions show that they have a truth which does not depend upon us. The essence of a circle, for example, and all other natures or essences and what we call eternal truths have an external cause of their constancy. This is the first proof in the order of knowledge. In the order of nature, the first proof of any existence is of ourselves from the fact that we think; but second, we realize that there is a variety in our thoughts, and that this variety does not come from ourselves, so there must be something external which causes the variety in our thoughts and sensations.[4]

However, Leibniz credits Foucher's Academic objections at this point. The soul in itself cannot cause the changes so there must be an outside reason for them, but from this only two things follow: 1) that

---

[1] Leibniz, Gottfried Wilhelm, *Nouveaux essais sur l'entendement par l'auteur du Système de l'harmonie preestablie* in *Schriften*, ed. Gerhardt, V, 355.

[2] Letter of Leibniz to Foucher (1676), *Schriften*, ed. Gerhardt, I, 369.

[3] *Ibid.*

[4] *Ibid.*, 370.

there is a connection in our appearances which allows us to predict future appearances, and 2) that this connection must have a constant cause. "Mais de tout cela il ne s'ensuit pas à la rigueur qu'il y a de la matiere ou des corps, mais seulement qu'il y a quelque chose qui nous presente des apparences bien suivies." [1] All could be a dream caused by a demon. Hence, we do not know the essence of what is external. Leibniz suspects that it is impossible for us to penetrate to such truths, knowledge of which would approach "de la vision beatifique." Descartes' distinction between body and soul is thus well-made, for though we cannot doubt that there is something external causing our thoughts and sensations, we can doubt whether or not it is something so utterly different from the soul as matter is. As for the demon, there is no need to prove the existence of God as Descartes does to find a non-deceiving being, "puisqu'il est en nostre pouvoir de nous detromper dans beaucoup de choses, et au moins sur les plus importantes." [2]

The first letter we have from Foucher to Leibniz is of 1678 and is not an answer to the above. Hence we must make our remarks by drawing from what Foucher has said elsewhere. It is first quite apparent that there is hardly any disagreement between Foucher and Leibniz. The proofs Leibniz offers for the existence of an external world are those Foucher admits in the *Apologie*. It is probable that Foucher never did deny the existence of *something* external; Leibniz's remarks about mathematical truths and the essence of body makes it clear that he realizes that Foucher's real concern is with how we can be assured of truths about this external world which has been proved to exist. And in this first letter he goes as far as Foucher ever did toward a statement that such knowledge is impossible for man. He does, later, however, venture an opinion; and it may be that those truths of reason which Foucher doubted "un peau trop" were the ones which Leibniz felt constraining him to offer his New System. It probably derives from his unconcern about whether or not life is a dream, for even dreams are real and have external causes.[3] Foucher never mentions the demon and hardly recognizes such depths of doubt, perhaps because it is irreverent speculation.

[1] *Ibid.*, 372–373.

[2] *Ibid.*, 373–374.

[3] Leibniz, Gottfried Wilhelm, "De Modo Distinguendi Phaenomena Realia ab Imaginariis" in *Schriften*, ed. Gerhardt, VII, 319–322. Quotations are from the English translation: "On the Method of Distinguishing Real from Imaginary Phenomena" in *Philosophical Papers and Letters*, Translated by Leroy E. Loemker, 2 volumes with continuous pagination (Chicago: University of Chicago Press, 1956), 604.

Probably in 1685 Foucher sent Leibniz his *Réponse* to Desgabets and his volume of verse, *De la Sagesse des anciens*.[1] Leibniz was enchanted and replied that there was much of interest in the ancients, suggesting that Foucher compose a synthesis of all that is valuable in them. He thinks the Academic philosophy, "qui est la connoissance des foiblesses de nostre raison, est bonne pour les commencemens." And since we are always beginning in religion, he agrees that it is best there to submit reason to authority.

Mais en matiere de connoissances humaines il faut tacher d'avancer, et quand même ce ne seroit qu'en establissant beaucoup de choses sur quelque peu de suppositions, cela ne laisseroit pas d'estre utile, car au moins nous scaurons qu'il ne nous reste qu'à prouver ce peu de suppositions pour parvenir à une pleine demonstration, et en attendant, nous aurons au moins des verités hypothetiques, et nous sortirions de la confusion des disputes. C'est la methode des Geometres.[2]

We need only begin by putting in geometric order such assumptions as the principle of contradiction and that in all true propositions the predicate is in the subject. Then we could begin to end disputes by demonstrations.

Il est même constant qu'on doit supposer certaines verités, ou renoncer à toute esperance de faire des demonstrations, car les preuves ne sçauroient aller à l'infini. Il ne faut rien demander qui soit impossible, autrement ce seroit témoigner qu'on ne recherche pas serieusement la verité.[3]

It would be to abuse words to say that such necessary propositions as that two contradictories cannot be true, and that what implies a contradiction cannot be, were established by free decree. He quibbles that Foucher even supposes them in writing and reasoning.[4] The rest of this letter contains an outline of Leibniz's New System. If Foucher ever answered it, Leibniz never received the letter.[5] It is questionable what Foucher could have said to the above. Leibniz's "assumptions" are all either identical propositions or reducible to identical propositions. The first, upon which all demonstrations are to rest, is the principle of contradiction which is his logical criterion of truth. It is psychologically impossible to doubt the principle of contradiction.

---

[1] Letter of Foucher to Leibniz (1685?), *Schriften*, ed. Gerhardt, I, 379.
[2] Letter of Leibniz to Foucher (1686), *Ibid.*, 381.
[3] *Ibid.*, 382.
[4] *Ibid.*, 383.
[5] Leibniz, Gottfried Wilhelm, "Eclaircissement du nouveau systeme de la communication des substances, pour servir de reponse à ce qui en a été dit dans le journal du 12 sept. 1695," *Journal des sçavans* (Amsterdam) XXIV (2 & 9 avril 1696), 255.

Foucher agrees to the validity of both of these criteria of truth. He does not ask that Leibniz's assumptions be proved by truths pushed back to infinity. He agrees to the *internal* truth of such deductive systems. Leibniz is merely showing his impatience. He is offering a criterion for proving something about the external world, while at the same time he recognizes its inadequacy. He says that since eternal truths have an external cause, this cause must be like them, and then we can go on to deduce further truths about the external world. But he has already said that knowledge of the existence of an external cause allows us no speculation about the essence of that cause. It is just this leap he is steeling himself to make, urging Foucher to join him. Foucher steadfastly refuses to decide upon a question for which he sees insufficient evidence.

In the remainder of the correspondence, each reiterates his major points. Leibniz agrees that the laws of the Academics "sont celles de la veritable Logique," but that in practice one must build.[1] Foucher is pleased that Leibniz continues to agree that the essence of matter, that is, the external cause of our sensations, is not extension.[2] He warns that all our conclusions are finite, for our souls are, and our ideas are only "facons d'estre de nostre ame."[3] Leibniz returns that it is true a few people should search for final proofs, but urges Foucher to make it clear that the Academics are not against advancement in science. The difficulties of Sextus Empiricus are not to be scorned, but practical progress can be made in science even when these difficulties are not resolved. He praises Foucher's *Apologie*, but adds, somewhat ironically, perhaps, that he wishes that to set a good example Foucher had given an examination and demonstration of some accepted axioms to commence the great search for truth.[4]

Leibniz agrees that some mathematical concepts are false in that things could not exist which answer to them. There are no mathematical points, and so on. But of them he says, "il y a certaines faussetés utiles pour trouver la verité." [5] The remark is equivocal. If he means the internal truths of mathematics, then obviously; but then they are not "faussetés." And if he means that concepts which cannot be true about the external world can lead us to truths about the external world, he has at least not satisfied Foucher. Foucher responds by

---

[1] Letter of Leibniz to Foucher (1687?), *Schriften* ed. Gerhardt, I, 390.
[2] Letter of Foucher to Leibniz (Paris, 30 mai 1691), *ibid.*, 399.
[3] Letter of Foucher to Leibniz (Paris, 31 decembre 1691), *ibid.*, 401.
[4] Letter of Leibniz to Foucher (janvier 1692), *ibid.*, 402.
[5] *Ibid.*, 406.

saying that the Academics doubt only "des propositions non demonstra-
tives."

Je consens que l'on démontre tant que l'on voudra les secondes veritez, en
les reduisant dans leurs principes immediatement, mais cela n'empesche
pas qu'il ne faille une fois pour le moins, aller depuis les derniers principes
jusqu'aux premiers, et vice versa.[1]

The demonstration Foucher wants is that showing one these "secondes
veritez" apply to the external world, and this is just the point upon
which Leibniz has strongly doubted that any demonstration can ever
be given. Foucher stops at that point; the "vice versa" in the last
quotation is impossible since the reduction has not been given.
Leibniz continues to cede the point. "Le meilleur seroit de reduire
tout aux premieres verités"; he says, "mais en attendant il sera tous-
jours bon de prendre les secondes qu'on attrape en chemin." [2] To this
Foucher responds with the dogmas of the Academics, insisting that
they do not doubt immediate experience and are not against progress
in science based on sense experience. But one should be careful not to
allow oneself to be led into dogmatism about the external world.[3]
This is what Foucher is afraid Leibniz has done in his New System.

   Foucher in a letter probably written in 1685 says he would like to
see a personal philosophy from Leibniz.[4] Leibniz responds in 1686 in
the course of a long letter commenting on Foucher's *Réponse* to Desgabets. In agreeing with Foucher's doubt that body and spirit could
interact, Leibniz offers his own view which seems necessary to him:

Je croy que toute substance individuelle exprime l'univers tout entier à sa
maniere, et que son estat suivant est une suite (quoyque souvent libre) de son
estat precedent, comme s'il n'y avoit que Dieu et Elle au monde; mais
comme toutes les substances sont une production continuelle de souverain
Estre, et experiment le même univers ou les mêmes phenomenes, elles
s'entraccordent exactement, et cela nous fait dire que l'une agit sur l'autre,
parce que l'une exprime plus distinctement que l'autre la cause ou raison
des changemens, à peu pres comme nous attribuons le mouvement plus
tost au vaisseau qu'à toute le mer, et cela avec raison.[5]

The external world can be explained mathematically and mechanically, of course, and this is how science should be done; but this does
not mean that the essence of matter is simply extension. There is

---

[1] Letter of Foucher to Leibniz (Paris, aoust 1692), *ibid.*, 407–408.
[2] Letter of Leibniz to Foucher (17/27 octobre 1692), *ibid.*, 410.
[3] Letter of Foucher to Leibniz (Paris, mars 1693), *ibid.*, 412–413.
[4] Letter of Foucher to Leibniz (1685?), *ibid.*, 380.
[5] Letter of Leibniz to Foucher (1686), *ibid.*, 382–383.

no real interaction among substances nor are there occasional causes:

je soutiens une concomitance ou accord de ce qui arrive dans les substances differentes, Dieu ayant créé l'ame d'abord, en sorte que tout cela luy arrive ou naisse de son fonds, sans qu'elle ait besoin de s'accommoder dans la suite au corps, non plus que le corps à l'ame. Chacun suivant ses loix, et l'un agissant librement, l'autre sans choix, se recontre l'un avec l'autre dans le mêmes phenomenes.[1]

Souls and matter, then, are in a pre-established harmony. The problem of their interaction is solved by showing how it is that one can talk about their interaction when in actuality there is none.

The New System is further developed in an extract of a letter to Foucher published in the *Journal des sçavans* of 27 June 1695 entitled "Sistême nouveau de la nature & de la communication des substances, aussi bien que de l'union qu'il y a entre l'ame & le corps". [2] Leibniz tells how as a young man he was a confirmed mechanist who scorned Scholastic faculties and forms. After many years of meditation, however, he found that the mechanical principle of extended matter is not enough for explanatory purposes. One needs also a metaphysical notion of force which can act as a principle of unity among extended things; such force or power of action is something like a soul with sentiment and appetite. It is a substantial form, but not such as is to be used to explain particular problems in physics for which mechanical principles are still sufficient. These primitive forms are the indivisible sources of activity.[3] They are metaphysical points which by their unifying activity constitute the only real substances, "et sans eux il n'y aurait rien de réel, puisque, sans les véritables unités, il n'y aurait point de multitude." [4] Leibniz then goes on to explain how God has created souls and bodies so that, with no interaction whatsoever, each is in perfect harmony in its actions with all the others by following its own laws. And "c'est ce rapport mutuel réglé par avance dans chaque substance de l'univers, qui produit ce que nous appelons leur communication, et qui fait uniquement l'union de l'âme et du corps." By its immediate presence, the soul is the substantial form which unifies the parts of the body.[5]

[1] *Ibid.*, 383.
[2] Leibniz, Gottfried Wilhelm, "Sistême nouveau de la nature & de la communication des substances, aussi bien que de l'union qu'il y a entre l'ame & le corps. Par M. D. L.," *Journal des sçavans* (Amsterdam), XXIII (27 juin & 4 juillet 1695), 444–454, 455–462. The page references which follow are to the more easily available reprint of this article in: *Oeuvres philosophiques de Leibniz*, ed. Janet, Paul (Paris: Felix Alcan, 1900), I, 635–644.
[3] *Ibid.*, 636–637.
[4] *Ibid.*, 640.
[5] *Ibid.*, 641–642.

Leibniz pleads that it is a quite plausible hypothesis. God could give these substances – metaphysical points – such natures or internal forces as to produce in themselves all the appearances they will ever have without the intervention of any other creature. He stresses that ordinary manners of speaking can be preserved, and that ordinary explanations in physics are still to be made on the principles of mechanics. But, "comme la masse matérielle n'est pas une substance,"[1] it is clear that there is no causal interaction among material things. The primary source of all action, of course, is God; the only secondary sources of action are the metaphysical points or souls which express the universe from different points of view by producing their own perceptions. These substantial forms also unify material bodies.

The "Réponse de M.S.F. à M.B.Z. sur son nouveau sisteme de la communication des substances" appeared in the *Journal des sçavans* of 12 September 1695.[2] Foucher agrees that something like Scholastic forms are necessary for the individuation of unities. He also admits that God could adjust things as Leibniz suggests. Then he says:

Mais, après tout, à quoi peut servir tout ce grand artifice dans les substances, sinon pour faire croire que les unes agissent sur les autres, quoique cela ne soit pas?

Leibniz's system is, alas, no better than the Cartesians'. Of what good or need is body in such a system? Leibniz too has "des corps inutiles que l'esprit ne saurait ni remuer ni connaître." The Cartesians, at least, are reduced to saying what they do because they develop their system in order to save the principle that there is nothing in common between spiritual and corporeal substances. To Leibniz Foucher says, "Mais vous, Monsieur, qui pourriez vous en démêler par d'autres voies, je m'étonne de ce que vous vous embarrassez de leurs difficultés." Foucher is not misled by Leibniz's technical adjustments. If occasionalism is to be rejected "parce qu'il suppose inutilement que Dieu considérant les mouvements qu'il produit lui-même dans le corps," then what better is a system where the adjustments are made all at once? [3]

---

[1] *Ibid.*, 642–644.
[2] Foucher, Simon, "Réponse de M. S. F. à M. de L. B. Z. sur son nouveau sisteme de la communication des substances, proposé dans les journaux du 27 juin & 4 juillet 1695," *Journal des sçavans* (Amsterdam), XXIII (12 septembre 1695), 639–645. Page references which follow are to *Oeuvres philosophiques de Leibniz*, I, ed. Janet, Paul (Paris: Felix Alcan, 1900).
[3] *Ibid.*, 647.

Foucher points out that we still do not know the nature of matter. He feels that Leibniz has missed a sterling opportunity to adjust his system to the facts of experience, and we do experience the interaction of soul and body, whatever either may be essentially. Since Leibniz is not committed to the utter difference of soul and body, Foucher cannot understand why he resorts to occasionalism, pre-established though it be. Hence, Foucher offers a suggestion to repair Leibniz's system.

Car qui est-ce qui ne conçoit qu'une balance étant en équilibre et sans action, si on ajoute un poids nouveau à l'un des côtés, incontinent on voit du mouvement, et l'un des contrepoids fait monter l'autre, malgré l'effort qu'il fait pour descendre. Vous concevez que les êtres materiéls sont capables d'efforts et de mouvement; et il s'ensuit fort naturellement que le plus grand effort doit surmonter le plus faible. D'autre part, vous reconnaissez aussi que les êtres spirituels peuvent faire des efforts; et comme il n'y a point d'effort qui ne suppose quelque résistance, il est nécessaire ou que cette résistance se trouve plus forte ou plus faible; si plus forte, elle surmonte; si plus faible, elle cède. Or, il n'est pas impossible que l'esprit faisant effort pour mouvoir le corps, le trouve muni d'un effort contraire qui lui résiste tantôt plus, tantôt moins, et cela suffit pour faire qu'il en souffre. C'est ainsi que St. Augustin explique de dessein formé, dans ses livres de la musique, l'action des esprits sur les corps.[1]

Foucher closes his criticism by remarking that such questions should not be decided until first principles are established. Such questions are not insoluble, but they depend upon first finding "la marque in-faillible de la verité." [2] Once this tie between first principles and the external world is made, then one can proceed to demonstrate truths about the external world from these principles.

Leibniz presents an "Eclaircissement" to answer Foucher in the *Journal des sçavans* for 2 and 9 April 1696.[3] He insists that his is no arbitrary hypothesis; he is led to it as the only correct one. Hence it is beside the point to ask what its use is, since it is the way things are; one does not ask, e.g., what purpose the incommensurability of the side with the diagonal of a triangle serves. However, one is constrained to accept the correspondence theory, because it

sert à expliquer la communication des substances, et l'union de l'âme avec le corps par les lois de la nature établies par avance, sans avoir recours ni

---

[1] *Ibid.*, 647–648.

[2] *Ibid.*, 648.

[3] Leibniz, Gottfried Wilhelm, "Eclaircissement du nouveau systeme de la communication des substances, pour servir de reponse à ce qui en a été dit dans le journal du 12 sept. 1695," *Journal des sçavans* (Amsterdam), XXIV (2 & 9 avril 1696), 255–258, 259–263. Page references which follow are to *Oeuvres*, I, ed. Janet.

à une transmission des espèces [Gassendi], qui est inconcevable, ni à un nouveau secours de Dieu [Malebranche], qui paraît peu convenable. Car il faut savoir que, comme il y a des lois de la nature dans la matière, il y en a aussi dans les âmes ou formes; et ces lois portent ce que je viens de dire.[1]

Body is not useless. "Dieu a voulu qu'il y eût plutôt plus que moins de substances, et qu'il a trouvé bon que ces modifications de l'âme répondissent à quelque chose de dehors." [2] It is simply God's design. And the soul does know these external bodies, though not through mutual influence. One can still speak of interaction, of course, if one remembers "que l'une est cause des changements dans l'autre en conséquence des lois de l'harmonie." [3] But he objects to the Cartesian notion of matter as inert extension, which *is* useless:

Je ne connais point ces masses vaines, inutiles et dans l'inaction, dont on parle. Il y a de l'action partout, et je l'établis plus que la philosophie reçue; parce que je crois qu'il n'y a point de corps sans mouvement, ni de substance sans effort.[4]

Even so, with such agreement with Foucher concerning the nature of body as opposed to the Cartesian notion, Leibniz fails to understand Foucher's criticism about saving principles.

Toutes les hypothèses sont faites exprès, et tous les systèmes viennent après coup, pour sauver les phénomènes ou les apparences; mais je ne vois pas quels sont les principes dont on dit que je suis prévenu, et que je veux sauver.[5]

Foucher had said simply that the appearances are that body and soul interact. Leibniz "saves" these appearances, not by blazing a new trail – or renewing an old one, Augustine's – but by clinging to the Malebranchian principle that there is no interaction between body and soul. Leibniz offers a new way of talking as though there is inter-action, which way of talking is inoffensive, if properly understood. But Foucher is not satisfied – as few people ever are initially – with new definitions which preserve the ordinary ways of talking. Leibniz so far misses the point as to go on to say: "Si cela veut dire que je suis porte à mon hypothèse encore par des raisons à priori, ou par de certains principes, comme cela est ainsi en effet; c'est plutôt une

---

[1] *Oeuvres*, I, ed. Janet, 650.
[2] *Ibid.*
[3] *Ibid.*, 651.
[4] *Ibid.*
[5] *Ibid.*

louange de l'hypothèse qu'une objection." [1] He goes on to explain how he has solved the problem of interaction between soul and body which has tumbled so many philosophers. Rather than taking Foucher's suggestion about the influence of forces upon each other on the principle that every effort requires a resistance, Leibniz explains again that for him the efforts are only internally in substances. Effort and resistance seemingly between substances can be explained by pre-established harmony of internal efforts, as is the seeming interaction between material things. [2]

He closes by saying that he believes he as much as anyone has followed what is good in Academic method. He thinks everyone should strive to conduct their demonstrations from first principles. [3] However, Leibniz himself does nothing about establishing the principles.

Foucher would certainly have replied had he been capable. He died on 27 April 1696. He surely would have pointed out the Malebranchian principle which determines Leibniz's new system, and would have urged him to cease attempting to save the appearances by building a system around the principle that there is no interaction among substances. Instead, Leibniz should strive to make intelligible what we all experience – the interaction of soul and body – by seeking knowledge of the essences of soul and body which make this interaction possible.

Before treating Leibniz's solutions to the epistemological problems raised by Foucher against Malebranche, we shall try to clear up a certain ambiguity concerning matter which has necessarily found its way into these last few pages. Leibniz uses the terms body and matter ambiguously in the writings we have been considering. The Cartesian notion is that matter is extension, to which Leibniz objects. But when he speaks of the pre-established harmony, he insists that there are substances – souls or forms – and then matter, which is not a substance, but which operates according to mechanical laws which are in harmony with the internal laws of the substances. He seems to be preserving occasionalism by reducing all the occasions to one. However, as we have seen him remark, he cannot conceive of this inert extended matter; there is action everywhere, so, presumably, there must be action in matter. Foucher has made the suggestion that the essences of souls and matter may be similar in being centers of force, and thereby can

[1] Ibid.
[2] Ibid., 652–653.
[3] Ibid., 652.

interact. While Leibniz rejects the interaction, there is some suggestion that he believes matter differs from the metaphysical points only by being extended centers of force.[1] This is unsatisfactory since Leibniz makes it clear in a paper written in the 1690's that he agrees with Foucher that extension is as phenomenal as color.[2] When he says in 1693 that all bodies are extended, he goes on to add that one should not confuse extension with the essence of substance.[3]

To determine Leibniz's position on matter at this time, we consider three papers: "First Truths" of around 1680–1684. "On the Method of Distinguishing Real from Imaginary Phenomena" of the early 1690's, and "On Nature Itself, or On the Inherent Force and Actions of Created Things" published in *Acta eruditorum* of September 1698.[4] In the first, "*There is no corporeal substance in which there is nothing but extension, or magnitude, figure, and their variations,*" is offered as a first truth. If it were not true, then there could be two exactly similar corporeal substances, which is absurd. "Hence it follows that there is something in corporeal substances analogous to the soul, which is commonly called form." [5] There are principles of action *in* corporeal substances. However, "Extension, motion, and bodies themselves, insofar as they consist in extension and motion alone, are not substances but true phenomena, like rainbows and parhelia." [6] The actual substance of body lacks extension. This opinion is repeated in the second paper where substances are said to have "metaphysical matter or passive power insofar as they express something confusedly; active, insofar as they express it distinctly." [7] In the third paper it is clearly stated that in all things there resides an "active creative force." Cartesian matter would be a mere "flux" and "nothing substantial."

---

[1] Loemker, *op. cit.*, 808.

[2] *Ibid.*, 606.

[3] *Oeuvres*, ed. Janet, I, 631.

[4] Leibniz, Gottfried Wilhelm, "Primae Veritates" in Couteret, Louis, *Opuscules et fragments inédits de Leibniz, extraits des manuscrits de la Bibliotheque royale de Hanovre* (Paris: Félix Alcan, 1903), 518–523. Quotations are from the English translation: "First Truths", (Ca. 1680–1684), *Philosophical Papers*, ed. Loemker, 411–417.

Leibniz, Gottfried Wilhelm, "De Modo Distinguendi Phaenomena Realia ab Imaginariis" in Gerhardt, *op. cit.*, VII, 319–322. Quotations are from the English translation: "On the Method of Distinguishing Real from Imaginary Phenomena," (Date unknown), *Philosophical Papers*, ed. Loemker, 602–607.

Leibniz, Gottfried Wilhelm, "De Ipsi Natura, sive de Vi Insita, Actionibusque Creaturarum; pro Dynamicus suis confirmandis illustrandisque," *Acta eruditorum Lipsiensum* (septembre, 1698), 427–440. Quotations are from the English translation: "On Nature Itself, or on the Inherent Force and Actions of Created Things to Serve to Confirm and Illustrate the Author's Dynamics," *Philosophical Papers*, ed. Loemker, 808–824.

[5] "First Truths", *Philosophical Papers*, ed. Loemker, 416.

[6] *Ibid.*, 417.

[7] "On the Method," *Philosophical Papers*, ed. Loemker, 607.

This is because the "extension, or the geometric nature of a body, taken alone contains nothing from which action and motion can arise." [1] And whatever does not act has no reason for existence, hence extension does not exist as a substance.[2] From these passages it is seen that Leibniz believes that material substances are nothing more than centers of power, while all that the Cartesians call matter is merely phenomenal. However, the kinds of power or force must be determined. The natural inertia of bodies indicates that there is a primary matter or mass which is a "passive force of resistance."[3] Activity cannot arise from this passive force, so there must be joined to it "a primitive motive force which, superadded to extension, or what is merely geometrical, and mass, or what is merely material, always acts indeed and yet is modified in various ways by the concourse of bodies, through a conatus or impetus." Leibniz goes on to say:

It is this substantial principle itself which is called the *soul* in living beings and *substantial form* in other beings, and inasmuch as it truly constitutes one substance with matter, or a unit in itself, it makes up what I call a monad. For if these true and real unities were dispensed with, only beings through aggregation would remain; indeed, it would follow that there would be left no true beings within bodies. For even though there are atoms of substance, namely, my monads, which lack parts, there are no atoms of mass or of minimum extension, or any last elements, since a continuum is not composed of points. Furthermore, there is no being that is greatest in mass or infinite in extension, even if there are always things greater than any given things; there is only a being greatest in intension of perfection or infinite in power.[4]

Hence, while Leibniz says that extension as such is not a substance, he retains the elements of the Cartesian dualism by making a radical distinction between passive centers of force – matter – which merely resist, and active centers of force which are souls or substantial forms, the unifying principles of material things. The union of these two very different forces can be only a manner of speaking derived from the harmony of their actions and passions established by God. Leibniz's reasoning from the passivity of matter to the necessity of an active monad, is, then, at least half sophistical. For the monads in no way activate matter; they merely reel off their own pictures of the world, while matter operates under another set of laws established by God. Monads seem necessary only as unifying principles, and even this

[1] "On Nature Itself," *Philosophical Papers*, ed. Loemker, 817.
[2] *Ibid.*, 824.
[3] The universe is a *plenum*. "First Truths," *Philosophical Papers*, ed. Loemker, 415.
[4] "On Nature Itself," *Philosophical Papers*, ed. Loemker, 818–819.

implies no real interaction. Foucher might well ask at this point how these monads can be the substantial forms of material things when the union is merely verbal. He would probably go on to point out that the distinction between passive and active centers of force which we have stressed to make the analogy to the Cartesian dualism is not really so stringent, for they both are centers of force. Where souls and bodies both are composed of centers of force, Foucher would say, there is a possibility of explaining the interaction between them which everyone experiences. Leibniz himself, though he would deny the interaction, can mean the difference only as a matter of degree, for whatever completely lacks active force is not a substance.[1]

Leibniz's New System was developed while he was in active correspondence with Foucher. We shall now consider the development of Leibniz's specific answers to Foucher's objections to the Cartesian way of ideas.

Leibniz made several notes concerning ideas in the margins of Foucher's *Réponse* to Desgabets. Concerning page 30 of the *Réponse*, Leibniz comments: "Idea est id quo perceptio sive cogitatio una ab alia differt ratione objeti." [2] The term idea stands either for the quality or form of thought, that is, a modification of the soul, or it stands for the immediate object of perception which is not a modification of the soul. Plato and Malebranche seem to hold the second view, and Leibniz says concerning page 39 of the *Réponse* that in the sense that there is an immediate cause from God of ideas, "il se peut que nous voyions tout en Dieu, et que les idées ou objets immédiés soyent les attributs de Dieu mesme." [3] He says that this is an imprecise way of speaking, however. As for representative ideas, Leibniz comments concerning page 33 of the *Reponse:*

Les idées, quoy qu'elles ne soyent point étendues, peuvent servir à connoistre l'étendue, et il peut y avoir un rapport entre ce qui est étendue et ce qui ne l'est pas, comme par exemple, entre l'angle et l'arc qui le mesure." [4]

In 1678 Leibniz wrote a short paper entitled "What is an idea?"

---

[1] *Ibid.*, 824.

[2] Leibniz, Gottfried Wilhelm, "Excerpta ex notis meis inauguralibus ad Fucherii responsionem in Malebranchium critica", Appendice VI in Rabbe, Félix, *Étude philosophique, L'Abbé Simon Foucher chanoine de la Sainte Chapelle de Dijon* (Paris: Didier, 1867), XLI. Some of these notes are translated: "Notes on the Reply of Foucher to the Criticism of his Criticism of the *Recherche de la verité*" (1676) in *Philosophical Papers*, ed. Loemker, 241. Loemker's translation of the quoted passage is: "An idea is that by which one perception of thought differs from another with respect to its object."

[3] Rabbe, *op. cit.*, XLI.

[4] *Ibid.*

"First of all," he says, "by the term *idea* we understand *something which is in our mind*." [1] This eliminates brain traces; thoughts, perceptions, and affections are also eliminated because "*an idea consists, not in some act, but in the faculty of thinking,* and we are said to have an idea of a thing even if we do not think of it, if only, on a given occasion, we can think of it." [2] This does not seem completely satisfactory, for there are methods by which one can reach objects without having ideas of them. So Leibniz says an idea must also express the thing. "That is said to express a thing in which there are relations [*habitudines*] which correspond to the relations of the thing expressed."[3] This can be done by models, the projection of solids on a plane, speech, symbols, and equations.

What is common to all these expressions is that we can pass from a consideration of the relations in the expression to a knowledge of the corresponding properties of the thing expressed. Hence it is clearly not necessary for that which expresses to be similar to the thing expressed, if only a certain analogy is maintained between the relations.[4]

Expressions based in nature require some similarity, such as between a large and small circle, or some connective relation as between a circle and an ellipse; arbitrary relations, such as between words and ideas, do not. Leibniz says that "every entire effect represents the whole cause, for I can always pass from the knowledge of such an effect to a knowledge of its cause. So, too, the deeds of each one represent his mind, and in a way the world itself represents God." [5] Ideas seem to be natural expressions such as that between a circle and an ellipse.

That the ideas of things are in us means therefore nothing but that God, the creator alike of the things and of the mind, has impressed a power of thinking upon the mind so that it can by its own operations produce ideas which correspond perfectly to what follows from the nature of things. Although, therefore, the idea of a circle is not similar to the circle, truths can be derived from it which would be confirmed beyond doubt by investigating a real circle.[6]

It will be noted here, as well as in the example of the arc and angle, that Leibniz takes "similar" to mean "exact resemblance."

[1] Leibniz Gottfried, Wilhelm, "Quid sit Idea" in *Schriften*, ed. Gerhardt, VII, 263–264. Quotations are from the English translation: "What is an Idea?," (1678), *Philosophical Papers*, ed. Loemker, 317.
[2] *Ibid.*
[3] *Ibid.*, 318.
[4] *Ibid.*
[5] *Ibid.*, 318–319.
[6] *Ibid.*, 319.

A short essay by Leibniz, "Meditations on Knowledge, Truth, and Ideas," appears in the *Acta eruditorum* of November 1684.[1] In it he distinguishes between obscure concepts such as when one remembers seeing a flower in a place but not which flower, and distinct concepts which contain sufficient marks to distinguish an object from all others. Of distinct concepts "we have a *nominal definition*, which is nothing but the enumeration of sufficient marks." [2] Primitive concepts are also distinct, though indefinable, as they are their own marks. "*Real definitions*" are those "through which the possibility of a thing is ascertained," and hence are necessary for perfect knowledge. "An idea is true when the concept is possible; it is false when it implies a contradiction." [3] The goal in knowledge is to reduce all real definitions to indefinable, possible, primitive concepts upon which they depend. Leibniz is doubtful if this can ever be completely accomplished. There is such difficulty in determining which concepts are clear and distinct that it is obvious that the Cartesian principle is defective which states that whatever is clearly and distinctly perceived is true.[4]

Leibniz allows that:

It can be said that we see all things in God, but it must be understood that, even if we saw all things in God, it would still be necessary to have our own ideas also, not in the sense of some kind of little copies, but as affections or modifications of our mind, corresponding to the very object we perceive in God. For, whenever thoughts succeed each other, some change occurs in our mind. There are also ideas in our mind of things of which we are not actually thinking, as the figure of Hercules is in the rough marble.[5]

Hence, even if there are ideas in God, we perceive those ideas by our own ideas, just as we are said to perceive material things by ideas. Whatever is external must be known by way of an idea in the soul.

Leibniz concludes with a remark on the perception of sensible qualities.

Moreover, when we perceive colors or odors, we are having nothing but a perception of figures and motions, but of figures and motions so complex and minute that our mind in its present state is incapable of observing each distinctly and therefore fails to notice that its perception is compounded of

---

[1] Leibniz, Gottfried Wilhelm, "Meditationes de Cognitione, Veritate et Ideis," *Schriften*, ed. Gerhardt, IV, 422–426. Quotations are from the English translation: "Meditations on Knowledge, Truth, and Ideas," *Acta eruditorum Lipsiensum*, (novembre 1684), *Philosophical Papers*, ed. Loemker, 448–481.

[2] *Ibid.*, 449.

[3] *Ibid.*, 452.

[4] *Ibid.*, 452–453.

[5] *Ibid.*, 454.

single perceptions of exceedingly small figures and motions. So when we mix yellow and blue powders and perceive a green color, we are in fact sensing nothing but yellow and blue thoroughly mixed; but we do not notice this and so assume some new nature instead.[1]

This passage requires interpretation, for figure and motion are just as "apparent" or sensible for Leibniz as are colors and other sensible qualities. Leibniz seems to be saying that if our senses were fine enough, we would have sensations of nothing but figures and motions. These two qualities are enough for mechanical physics, and no doubt it is because of this that Leibniz makes such a distinction between primary and secondary qualities. In a more complete analysis he would have to go on to say that figure and motion are also secondary, in the sense that they are only effects of substances which are active centers of force.[2]

From this set of papers, then, we can conclude that for Leibniz an idea is a modification of the soul which expresses its object. This expression is due to no similarity between idea and object, but to a correspondence or analogy of relations which are apparent both in the idea and in the object. Whatever we know is known by an idea. An idea is true if it is possible, that is, if it does not contain a contradiction; but to know if an idea really corresponds to its object one would have to compare idea and object, which is impossible. We are assured of this correspondence, however, by the fact that God made both ideas and objects, and He made ideas to express objects.

Two years after publishing on ideas in the *Acta eruditorum* Leibniz wrote Foucher a long letter discussing Foucher's *Réponse* to Desgabets. It is in agreeing with Foucher's doubts about the interaction between Cartesian body and soul that Leibniz outlines his New System. Concerning the sixth assumption, that our ideas need not resemble the objects they represent, Leibniz agrees with Malebranche. He says that:

il n'est pas necessaire que ce que nous concevons des choses hors de nous, leur soit parfaitement semblable, mais qu'il les exprime, comme une Ellipse exprime un cercle vu de travers, en sort qu'à chaque point du cercle il en reponde un de l'Ellipse et vice versa, suivant une certaine loy de rapport. Car comme j'ay déja dit, chaque substance individuelle exprime l'univers à sa maniere, à peu pres comme une même ville est exprimée diversement selon les differens points de veue.[3]

[1] *Ibid.*
[2] "On the Method," *Philosophical Papers*, ed. Loemker, 606–607.
[3] Letter of Leibniz to Foucher (1686), *Schriften*, ed. Gerhardt, I, 383.

He goes on to explain that God has resolved it this way. He says the way to determine if extension is a phenomenon like color is to find out whether there is something more which is the essence of material substance. As we have seen, he discovers substance to be a center of force. Hence, he offers an argument different from Foucher's for the relegation of extension to the phenomenal realm: neither extension nor other sensible qualities are the essence of matter. For further discussion, Leibniz refers Foucher to the *Acta eruditorum* article.[1]

On the occasion of receiving Part II of Foucher's *Apologie* in 1687, Leibniz continues to develop his answer to Foucher's problems. He finds that the truth is that "chaque substance (conjointement avec le concours de Dieu) est la cause réele immediate de ce qui se passe dans elle." [2] In a note written on his copy of the letter but not sent to Foucher, Leibniz says:

Je prouve mesme que l'estendu, la figure, et le mouvement enferment quelque chose d'imaginaire et d'apparent, et quoyqu'on les concoive plus distinctement que la couleur ou la chaleur, neantmoins, quand on pousse l'analyse aussi loin que j'ay fait, on trouve que ces notions ont encor quelque chose de confus, et que, sans supposer quelque substance qui consiste en quelque autre chose, elles seroient aussi imaginaires que les qualités sensibles, ou que les songes bien reglés. Car par le mouvement en luy même, on ne sçauroit determiner à quel sujet il appartient; et je tiens pour demonstrable qu'il n'y a nulle figure exacte dans les corps.[3]

Leibniz has, then, at least three reasons different from Foucher's for saying that the primary qualities do not actually belong to material substance as the Cartesians claim: 1) extension is not the essence of matter, 2) all appearances in the soul are caused by the soul, and 3) the notions of extension, figure, and movement are confused. Even so, it is still permissible and even imperative to do physics according to mechanical principles; as always, it is all right to talk about physical things if one understands the locution. One of the virtues Leibniz finds in his system is that with it one can still talk in ordinary ways.[4]

Leibniz and Foucher, we see, have many points of agreement. They both disagree with the Cartesians on the essences of substances and mistrust the Cartesian principle of clearness and distinctness as a criterion for true ideas. Foucher feels that Leibniz's system of active forces retains too many of the elements of occasionalism, but sees in it

---

[1] *Ibid.*, 384.
[2] Letter of Leibniz to Foucher (1687?), *Ibid.*, 391.
[3] *Ibid.*, 392.
[4] "On Nature Itself," *Philosophical Papers*, ed. Loemker, 817: "Sistème nouveau," *Oeuvres*, ed. Janet, I, 643.

a possible way of making intelligible the interaction between body and soul that we all experience. Leibniz offers the principle of contradiction as the criterion of the truth of ideas, but recognizes with Foucher that this gives only an internal truth and is not a criterion for determining if ideas actually apply to external things. Leibniz agrees that there is a need to search for this ultimate criterion to establish first principles, and Foucher agrees that science can progress by hypothetical systems without it. Leibniz does not insist that the great success of hypothetical science means that it could be absolutely certain (as does Régis),[1] and Foucher does not insist that the uncertainty of first principles means that scientific research should be abandoned (as does La Mothe Le Vayer).[2] But Foucher does believe that the proper work of a philosopher is to search for the criterion. Leibniz, on the other hand, believes that he has reduced all to one principle – the principle of contradiction [3] – and hence is justified in concerning himself with hypothetical science. There remains only the establishment of this one principle to make science certain, and there is need of only a few workers – such as Foucher – to aim toward this goal.

Had Foucher lived to criticize Leibniz's doctrine of ideas, there would probably have been less agreement. He would have pointed out that an arc and a circle, and a circle and an ellipse, are all extended; thus the analogy to idea and material thing cannot hold. He would agree that an idea as a modification of the soul is necessary to know an external idea in God, but, granting the possibility of resemblance between these two spiritual ideas, the problem of resemblance with a material thing would still remain. He would agree that since God is the primary cause of everything, one can, in a manner of speaking,[4] say that we see all things in God. But he would say that Leibniz is, like Malebranche, only making a pious remark which explains nothing when he says that God makes us have ideas which express their objects. Rather, he would probably say, the fact that all substances are centers of force makes it possible in Leibniz's system for modifications of one substance to resemble those of another. Just as he suggests that Leibniz seems to have a notion of substance which would allow him to explain interaction between substances intelligibly (though he does not do it), so also might he suggest that the system allows for the possibility that

[1] See Chapter V, p. 76, n.l.
[2] Popkin, Richard H., *The History of Scepticism from Erasmus to Descartes* (Assen: Van Gorcum, 1960; revised edition, 1964), 93-94.
[3] Letter of Leibniz to Foucher (1687?), *Schriften*, ed Gerhardt, I, 393.
[4] Letter of Foucher to Leibniz (Paris: 28 avril 1695), *ibid.*, 423.

ideas could resemble and hence truly represent their objects. Leibniz solves Foucher's problem by eliminating extension from matter; Foucher might continue to worry about extension being in the soul.

In concluding this chapter it must be remarked that however favorable Foucher is to Leibniz's system, he would never accept it until he finds the criterion which assures him that Leibniz's notion of the essence of substance really applies to external substances. Leibniz, if anything, is more doubtful that this ultimate grounding of first principles can ever be accomplished than is Foucher.[1]

Foucher developed his objections to Cartesianism in his criticisms of Malebranche, in his correspondence with Leibniz, and in his dispute with Desgabets. We have seen how far-reaching these objections are. They extend to any system which retains something of the Cartesian dualism. They are thus easily applicable to Malebranche's system and retain their force against Leibniz's New System.

---

[1] Letter of Leibniz to Foucher (1676), *ibid.*, 373.

# CHAPTER IX

# CONCLUSION

The downfall of Cartesianism in the late 17th century has now been traced to the inability of Cartesians to solve two major problems deriving from conflicts among their metaphysical principles: They could give philosophically satisfactory explanations neither of how minds can know material objects, nor of how mind and matter can causally interact.

The seat of the difficulties is Cartesian ontology, which is dualistic in two respects. First, there is a dualism of created substances, mind and matter, which differ in essence. Second, there is a dualism of types of ontological entities: whatever exists is either a substance or a modification of a substance. The primary Cartesian existents, then, are (besides God) material things modified by size, shape, and motion or rest, and minds modified by sensations and ideas. Problems arose when the Cartesians attempted either to follow or to abandon the principles that essential likeness is necessary between cause and effect, and between idea and object, and that direct acquaintance is necessary for knowledge.

The attack upon Cartesian metaphysics began with consideration of a third aspect which is also dualistic, the epistemological distinction between ideas which represent their objects and sensations which are non-representative. Since sensations and ideas are all that is directly knowable for the Cartesians, they asserted that material things are known mediately by way of representative ideas. The major critic of this view, Foucher, believed that the representative aspect of ideas must be ontologically grounded. He first asserted that since both ideas and sensations are modifications of mind, either both must, or neither can, represent material objects. Foucher then went on to point out that *as* modifications of mind, ideas differ in essence from material objects and thus are ontologically unlike them. Since the only satisfactory ground he knew of for the representation of an object by an idea is that of essential likeness or resemblance between the two, Foucher concluded that material objects cannot be known by way of Cartesian ideas. Ideas cannot *represent* material objects because ideas do not *resemble* material objects. Foucher also insisted that there could be no causal interaction between unlike substances.

In response to Foucher's criticisms the orthodox Cartesians claimed that ideas represent material objects without resembling them. Desgabets, La Forge, Rohault, Régis, Le Grand, and Arnauld employed two arguments. They said either that representation by non-resembling ideas is fundamental and thus is not in need of explanation, or that while such representation is inexplicable, it is not impossible, Arnauld in particular defended the claim that it is of the nature of ideas to represent their objects without resembling them. However, even Arnauld's arguments ultimately reduced to the orthodox position that we cannot understand how it is done, but since God creates and knows both mind and matter, He can and certainly does make it so that mind knows matter. The orthodox Cartesians also admitted that causal interaction between unlike substances is inexplicable; they found support for interaction between mind and matter – as for non-resembling representation – only in the unknown ways of God.

Malebranche is one of the first major Cartesians to face these crucial systemic problems. In opposition to the orthodox Cartesians, Malebranche did not reject the causal and the epistemological likeness principles. Admitting that there can be no causal interaction between mind and matter, he developed occasionalism. And ideas presumably do resemble their objects in some manner, for they are the ideas by which God knows – and thus according to which he created – the world. Ideas are not modifications of mind, Malebranche contended, but are *in* God. Malebranche's doctrine of external ideas is problematic because he retained the traditional principle that whatever exists is either a substance or a modification, while trying to solve some and avoid other epistemological problems by insisting that ideas are neither. The orthodox Cartesians felt no need to explain how a mind could be directly acquainted with ideas which are modifications of the mind, but they had to call upon God to explain the representation by mental ideas of anything which is unlike ideas. Malebranche could not base direct acquaintance with external ideas upon the relation between a substance and its modifications, nor could he base representation upon the resemblance of such ideas to material objects. If external things must be known mediately, then knowledge of external ideas perhaps also needs mediation. And if external ideas are neither substances nor modifications, they certainly cannot resemble and thus represent material substances and modifications. Foucher, Leibniz, and Arnauld argued that the theory according to which we see all things in God can be viewed charitably only as an expression of piety; it offers no philosophical clarification or explanation of the issues at hand.

Foucher's criticisms of Cartesian metaphysics were fatal because even the orthodox Cartesians were strongly committed to the causal and epistemological likeness principles. This is most evident in their mechanical explanations of physical events, and in their agreement that resemblance between idea and object is the only *understandable* ground for representation of object by idea. The Cartesians admitted that the causal and epistemological issues were crucial. But whether they tried to adhere to the likeness principles (as did Malebranche) or tried to abandon them (as did the orthodox Cartesians), they still could not explain within the limits of Cartesian ontology how a mind could causally interact with and know material objects.

From the rich debris of continental metaphysics, Locke cobbled his own version of the way of ideas. He said that ideas resemble and thus represent primary qualities of material objects. A possible ontological ground for this resemblance was provided by his insistence that extension and thinking are not the essences of matter and mind, but are nothing more than modifications of unknown substances. Mind and matter might, after all, be essentially similar, and then interaction and representation could be explained. Foucher, Leibniz, and even Descartes had explored the possibilities of such a monistic solution; Spinoza, however, was the philosopher who developed – and was vilified for it – that way out. Locke's position, instead, made clearly evident the inadequacies of the way of representative ideas.

New developments in the way of ideas came by way of Malebranche, and Foucher through Bayle, in the philosophy of ideas of Berkeley. For Berkeley, nothing is like an idea but an idea, thus ideas are all that can be known by way of ideas. Though he eliminated matter (and thus found no problems of causal interaction between unlike substances), Berkeley retained the ontological dualism of *types* of existents, that is, substance and modification. And since he reasoned about ideas always as though they were modifications of the mind, he found the direct acquaintance of a mind with its own ideas unproblematic.

But Berkeley decided that ideas which are all passive cannot adequately resemble and thus represent active minds; there can be no ideas of, but only notions of, minds. Cartesian problems stemmed from unlike substances. The problems of Berkeley's doctrine of notions stemmed from his recognition of the unlikeness between substance and modification. Berkeley could not explain how we have knowledge of minds.

In the metaphysical systems of substance and modification into which they were introduced, Malebranchian external ideas and Berkeleian notions perform epistemological roles, but they have no ontological place. Malebranche sensed that ideas cannot be limited in their representative power by their ontological status if they are to perform in their epistemological role. But neither he nor Berkeley could break away from the use of ontological relations as ground for epistemological relations. Berkeley and the Cartesians were bound, in the last analysis, to the notion that ideas are (and must be) modifications of the mind, because only the relation of a substance to its modifications gives ontological support to the relation of direct acquaintance between a mind and its ideas.

Hume finally abandoned the whole of Cartesian ontology, both the dualism of substances, and the categories of substance and modification. He compressed the distinctions between Cartesian sensations and ideas, Malebranchian sensations and external ideas, and Berkeleian ideas and notions. As a *reductio*, he argued that if independent existence is the criterion of a substance, then his perceptions are substances. Though perceptions are all ontologically of the same kind and type, and though ideas represent by being like impressions, perceptions are neither substances nor modifications. Hume culminates a tradition of sceptical arguments by abandoning substance philosophy.

In a wider philosophical context, then, Cartesianism inherited the traditional likeness principles and the ontology of substance and modification; its inadequacies are germane to the modern failure of substance philosophy. In the narrower compass of the late 17th century, the dependence of Cartesians upon the ontology of substance and modification led to their inability to explain how causal interaction takes place between unlike substances, and how ideas make objects which are unlike them known. This inability deriving from conflicts among basic principles in the Cartesian system was the major philosophical reason for the downfall of Cartesianism.

## Appendix I

### A TABLE OF THE PRINCIPLES OF A LATE
### 17TH CENTURY CARTESIAN METAPHYSICAL SYSTEM

Ontologically, Cartesianism comprises:

(A)  God is an uncreated substance.
(B)  There is a dualism of two created substances which differ in essence: mind is *thinking*; matter is *extension*.
(C)  Volitions, passions, sensations, and ideas are the (only) modifications of mind.
(D)  Size, shape, and motion or rest are the (only) modifications of matter.
(E)  There is an all-inclusive ontological type-distinction between substance and modification: substance is dependent on nothing else (save God); modifications or properties are dependent upon substance.

There are three causal principles:

(F)  There is causal interaction between mind and matter.
(G)  Ideas and sensations are caused in some way by the interaction of matter and mind.
(H)  There must be essential likeness between a cause and its effect.

And five epistemological principles:

(I)  Ideas represent objects external to the mind.
(J)  Sensations do not represent objects external to the mind.
(K)  There must be essential likeness between an idea and its object.
(L)  Direct acquaintance is necessary for knowledge.
(M)  Objects external to the mind are known only by the mediate representation of ideas.


## Appendix II

### A SCHEMATIC OUTLINE OF FOUCHER'S CRITICISMS OF CARTESIANISM

(*1*)  (F) cannot be true because of (B) which precludes the possibility of (H) upon which (F) depends.
(*2*)  (B) cannot be true because (F) and (H) are true and (B) leads to (*1*).
(*3*)  (C) and (G) give no evidence for the distinction made in (I) and (J), but rather for the denial of this distinction.
(*4*)  Because of (B), (K) cannot be fulfilled, therefore (I) is impossible.

# BIBLIOGRAPHY

## BOOKS

ARNAULD, ANTOINE. *Défense de M. Arnauld, Docteur de Sorbonne, contre la réponse au livre des vraies & des fausses idées.* Cologne: Nicolas Schouten, 1684.

ARNAULD, ANTOINE. *La Logique, ou l'art de penser.* Paris: C. Saureux, 1662.

ARNAULD, ANTOINE. *Des Vrayes et des fausses idées, contre ce qu'enseigne l'auteur de la Recherche de la vérité.* Cologne: Nicolas Schouten, 1683.

ARNAULD, ANTOINE. *Oeuvres de Messire Antoine Arnauld, Docteur de la Maison et Societé de Sorbonne.* 43 Volumes. Paris: Sigismond d'Arnay & Cie., 1775–1783.

BAILLET, ADRIEN. *La Vie de Monsieur Descartes.* Paris: Daniel Horthemels, 1691.

BALZ, ALBERT G. A. *Cartesian Studies.* New York: Columbia University Press, 1951.

BARBER, W. H. *Leibniz in France from Arnauld to Voltaire, A Study in French Reactions to Leibnizianism, 1670–1760.* Oxford: Clarendon Press, 1955.

BAYLE, PIERRE. *Dictionnaire historique et critique.* Cinquième édition, revue, corrigée, et augmentée. 4 Volumes. Amsterdam: P. Brunel. 1740.

BEER, HENRY. *Du Scepticisme de Gassendi.* Traduction de Bernard Rochot. Paris: Albin Michel, 1960.

BELAVAL, YVON. *Leibniz critique de Descartes.* Paris: Gallimard, 1960.

BERKELEY, GEORGE. *The Works of George Berkeley, Bishop of Cloyne.* Edited by A. A. Luce and T. E. Jessop. 9 Volumes. London: Thomas Nelson and Sons, 1948–1957.

BOAS, GEORGE. *Dominant Themes of Modern Philosophy, A History.* New York: Ronald Press, 1957.

BONNO, GABRIEL. *Les Relations intellectuelles de Locke avec la France (d'après des documents inédits).* University of California Publications in Modern Philology, Volume 38, No. 2, 37–264. Berkeley and Los Angeles: University of California Press, 1955.

BOUILLIER, FRANCISQUE. *Histoire de la philosophie cartésienne.* 2 Volumes. Paris: Durand, 1854.

BRACKEN, HARRY M. *The Early Reception of Berkeley's Immaterialism: 1710–1733.* The Hague: Martinus Nijhoff, 1959; revised edition, 1965.

BRETT, G. S. *The Philosophy of Gassendi.* London: Macmillan, 1908.

BURTT, EDWIN ARTHUR. *The Metaphysical Foundations of Modern Physical Science*. Revised edition. New York: Harcourt, Brace and Co., and London: Kegan Paul, Trench, Trubner & Co., Ltd., 1932.

CASSIRER, ERNST. *Das Erkenntnisproblem in der Philosophie und Wissenschaft der Neueren Zeit*. 2 Volumes. Berlin: B. Cassirer, 1911.

CHURCH, RALPH WITHINGTON. *A Study in the Philosophy of Malebranche*. London: George Allen & Unwin, Ltd., 1931.

COUSIN, VICTOR. *Fragments philosophiques pour faire suite aux cours de l'histoire de la philosophie*. Quatrième édition. 4 Volumes. Paris: Ladrange et Didier, 1847.

CURTIS, S. J. *A Short History of Western Philosophy in the Middle Ages*. London: MacDonald & Co., Ltd., 1950.

DAMIRON, M. PH. *Essai sur l'histoire de la philosophie en France, au XVIIe siècle*. 2 volumes. Paris: L. Hachette, 1846.

DELBOS, VICTOR. *Étude de la philosophie de Malebranche*. Paris: Bloud & Gay, 1924.

DESCARTES, RENÉ. *Oeuvres de René Descartes*. Publiées par Charles Adam & Paul Tannery. 12 volumes. Paris: Léopold Cerf, 1897.

DESCARTES, RENÉ. *The Philosophical Works of Descartes*. Translated by Elizabeth S. Haldane & G. R. T. Ross. 2 volumes. Cambridge: Cambridge University Press, 1931; New York: Dover, 1955.

DESGABETS, ROBERT. *Critique de la Critique de la Recherche de la vérité, où l'on découvre le chemin qui conduit aux connoissances solides. Pour servir de réponse à la Lettre d'un académicien*. Paris: Jean Du Puis, 1675.

DU HAMEL, JEAN. *Lettre de Monsieur Du Hamel, Ancien Professeur de Philosophie de l'Université de Paris, pour servir de Replique à Monsieur Régis*. Paris: publisher unknown, 8 mars 1699.

DU HAMEL, JEAN. *Réflexions critiques sur le système cartésienne de la philosophie de Mr. Régis*. Paris: E. Couterot, 1692.

FONTENELLE, BERNARD LE BOVIER DE. *Oeuvres de Fontenelle*. Tome VI. Paris: Jean-Francois Bastien, 1790.

FOUCHER, SIMON. *Critique de la Recherche de la vérité où l'on examine en même-tems une partie des Principes de Mr Descartes. Lettre, par un Academicien*. Paris: Martin Coustelier, 1675.

FOUCHER, SIMON. *Dissertation sur la recherche de la verité, contenant l'apologie des academiciens, où l'on fait voir que leur maniere de philosopher est la plus utile pour la religion, & la plus conforme au bon sens, pour servir de Réponse à la Critique de la Critique, &c. avec plusieurs remarques sur les erreurs des sens & sur l'origine de la philosophie de Monsieur Descartes*. Paris: Estienne Michallet, 1687.

FOUCHER, SIMON. *Dissertations sur la recherche de la verité, contenant l'histoire et les principes de la philosophie des academiciens. Avec plusieurs réflexions sur les sentimens de M. Descartes*. Paris: Jean Anisson, 1693.

FOUCHER, SIMON. *Dissertations sur la recherche de la verité, ou sur la logique des academiciens*. Dijon: publisher unknown, 1673.

FOUCHER, SIMON. *Lettre sur la morale de Confucius, philosophe de la Chine*. Paris: Daniel Horthemels, 1668.

FOUCHER, SIMON. *Sur la Mort de la reine*. Paris: publisher unknown, 1666.

FOUCHER, SIMON. *Nouvelle dissertation sur la recherche de la verité, contenant la Reponse à la Critique de la Critique de la Recherche de la verité, où l'on découvre les erreurs des dogmatistes, tant anciens que nouveaux, avec une discution particuliere du grand principe des cartesiens.* Paris: Robert de la Caille, 1679.

FOUCHER, SIMON. *Nouvelle façon d'hygrometres.* Place and publisher unknown, 1672.

FOUCHER, SIMON. *Réponse à la Critique de la Critique de la Recherche de la vérité sur la philosophie des académiciens.* Paris: Robert de la Caille, 1676.

FOUCHER, SIMON. *Réponse pour la Critique à la Preface du second volume de la Recherche de la verité, où l'on examine le sentiment de M. Descartes touchant les idées, avec plusieurs remarques pour les sciences.* Paris: Charles Angot, 1676.

FOUCHER, SIMON. *De la Sagesse des anciens, où l'on fait voir que les principales maximes de leur morale ne sont pas contraires au christianisme.* Paris: Dezailliers, 1682.

FOUCHER, SIMON. *Traité des hygrometres ou machines pour mesurer la secheresse et l'humidité de l'air.* Paris: Estienne Michallet, 1686.

GALILEI, GALILEO. *Dialogues concerning Two New Sciences.* Translated by Henry Crew and Alfonso de Salvio. New York: Macmillan, 1914.

GALILEI, GALILEO. *Il Saggiatore nel quale con bilancia escuisita e giusta si ponderano le cose contenute nella libra astronomica e fillosofica* ... Rome: Giacomo Mascardi, 1923.

GASSENDI, PIERRE. *Dissertations en forme de paradoxes contre les aristotéliciens (Exercitationes Paradoxicæ Adversus Aristoteleos) Livres I et II.* Texte latin établi, traduit et annoté par Bernard Rochot. Paris: J. Vrin, 1959.

GILSON, ETIENNE. *Études sur le rôle de la pensée médiévale dans la formation du système cartésien.* Paris: J. Vrin, 1951.

GILSON, ETIENNE. *Index scolastico-cartésien.* Paris: Félix Alcan, 1913.

GOUHIER, HENRI. *La Pensée métaphysique de Descartes.* Paris: J. Vrin, 1962.

GOUHIER, HENRI. *La Philosophie de Malebranche et son expérience religieuse.* Paris: J. Vrin, 1948.

GOUHIER, HENRI. *La Vocation de Malebranche.* Paris: J. Vrin, 1926.

GUEROULT, MARTIAL. *Berkeley.* Paris: Aubier, 1956.

GUEROULT, MARTIAL. *Descartes selon l'ordre des raisons.* 2 volumes. Paris: Aubier, 1953.

GUEROULT, MARTIAL. *Malebranche.* 3 volumes. Paris: Aubier, 1955, 1958, 1959.

HUET, PIERRE-DANIEL. *Censura Philosophiæ Cartesianæ.* Paris: Horthemels, 1689.

HUME DAVID. *A Treatise of Human Nature.* Edited by L. A. Selby-Bigge. Oxford: Clarendon Press, 1955.

HUME, DAVID. *Enquiries concerning the Human Understanding and concerning the Principles of Morals.* Edited by L. A Selby-Bigge. Oxford: Clarendon Press, 1955.

KOYRÉ, A. *Etudes galiléennes:* I. *A l'aube de la science classique.* Paris: Hermann & Cie, 1939.

KREMER, ELMAR J. *Malebranche and Arnauld: The Controversy Over the Nature of Ideas.* New Haven: Yale University Ph.D. Dissertation, unpublished, 1961.

La Forge, Louis de. *Traité de l'âme humaine, de ses facultés et fonctions et de son union avec le corps, d'après les principes de Descartes.* Paris: Girard, 1666.

La Grange, Jean-Baptiste de. *Les Principes de la philosophie, contre les nouveaux philosophes Descartes, Rohault, Regius, Gassendi, le P. Maignon, &c.* 2 volumes. Paris: G. Josse, 1675.

La Grange, Jean-Baptiste de. *Traité des éléments et des météores, contre les nouveaux philosophes Descartes, Rohault, Gassendi, le P. Maignon, &c.* Paris: Vve Josse, 1679.

Laporte, Jean. *Etudes d'histoire de la philosophie française au XVIIe siècle.* Paris: J. Vrin, 1951.

Laporte, Jean. *Le Rationalisme de Descartes.* Paris: Presses Universitaires de France, 1950.

Le Grand, Antoine. *An Entire Body of Philosophy, According to the Principles of the Famous Renate des Cartes, in three Books: I. The Institution... II. The History of Nature... III. A Dissertation of the Want of Sense and Knowledge in Brute Animals...* London: Samuel Roycraft, 1694.

Leibniz, Gottfried Wilhelm. *Discours de métaphysique et Correspondance avec Arnauld.* Introduction, texte et commentaire par Georges Le Roy. Paris: J. Vrin, 1957.

Leibniz, Gottfried Wilhelm. *Oeuvres philosophiques de Leibniz.* Edited by Paul Janet. 2 volumes. Paris: Félix Alcan, 1900.

Leibniz, Gottfried Wilhelm. *Opuscules et fragments inédits de Leibniz, extraits des manuscrits de la Bibliotheque Royale de Hanovre.* Edited by Louis Couteret. Paris: Félix Alcan, 1903.

Leibniz, Gottfried Wilhelm. *Philosophical Papers and Letters.* 2 volumes. Translated and edited by Leroy E. Loemker. Chicago: University of Chicago Press, 1956.

Leibniz, Gottfried Wilhelm. *The Philosophical Works of Leibniz.* New Haven: Tuttle, Morehouse & Taylor, 1890.

Leibniz, Gottfried Wilhelm. *Die Philosophischen Schriften von Gottfried Wilhelm Leibniz.* Herausgegeben von C. J. Gerhardt. 7 volumes. Berlin: Weidmannsche, 1875.

Lemaire, Paul. *Le Cartésienisme chez les Bénédictins. Dom Robert Desgabets son système, son influence et son école, d'après plusieurs manuscrits et des documents rares ou inédits.* Paris: Félix Alcan, 1901.

Lenoble, Robert. *Mersenne ou la naissance du mécanisme.* Paris: J. Vrin, 1943.

Locke, John. *An Early Draft of Locke's Essay together with Excerpts from his Journals.* Edited by R. I. Aaron and Jocelyn Gibb. Oxford: Clarendon Press, 1936.

Locke, John. *An Essay concerning Human Understanding.* Edited by A. C. Fraser. 2 volumes. Oxford: Clarendon Press, 1894.

Lough, John. *Locke's Travels in France 1675–1679 as related in his Journals, Correspondence and other Papers.* Cambridge: University Press, 1953.

Luce, A. A. *Berkeley and Malebranche, A Study in the Origins of Berkeley's Thought.* London: Oxford University Press, 1934.

Luce, A. A. *Berkeley's Immaterialism.* London: Thomas Nelson and Sons, 1945.

Malebranche, Nicolas. *Oeuvres complètes.* 20 volumes. Direction: André Robinet. Paris: J. Vrin, 1958–

MALEBRANCHE, NICOLAS. *Oeuvres complètes de Malebranche.* Tome I. Edited by Désiré Roustan et Paul Schrecker. Paris: Boiven et Cie, 1938.

MALEBRANCHE, NICOLAS. *De la Recherche de la vérité où l'on traite de la nature de l'esprit de l'homme, et de l'usage qu'il en doit faire pour éviter l'erreur des sciences.* Introduction et Texte Établi par Geneviève Lewis. 3 Volumes. Paris: J. Vrin, 1945.

MALEBRANCHE, NICOLAS. *Recueil de toutes les réponses du père Malebranche, prestre de l'Oratoire, à Monsieur Arnaud, docteur de Sorbonne.* 4 volumes. Rotterdam: R. Leers, 1694.

MANDON, L. *Étude sur le Syntagma philosophicum de Gassendi.* Montpellier: Pierre Grollier, 1858.

MENAGE, GILLES. *Menagiana, ou les bons mots et remarques critiques, historiques, morales & d'érudition, de Monsieur Menage, recueillies par ses amis.* Nouvelle édition. 4 volumes. Paris: Veuve Delaulne, 1729.

MOUY, PAUL. *Le développement de la physique cartésienne, 1646–1712.* Paris: J. Vrin, 1934.

POPKIN, RICHARD H. *The History of Scepticism from Erasmus to Descartes.* Assen: Van Gorcum, 1960; revised edition, 1964.

RABBE, FELIX. *Étude philosophique. L'Abbé Simon Foucher chanoine de la Sainte Chapelle de Dijon.* Paris: Didier et Cie, 1867.

RÉGIS, PIERRE-SYLVAIN. *Réponse aux Réflexions critiques de M. Du Hamel sur le système cartésien de la philosophie de M. Régis.* Paris: J. Cusson, 1692.

RÉGIS, PIERRE-SYLVAIN. *Système de philosophie, contenant la logique, la métaphysique, la physique et la morale.* 3 volumes. Lyon: Denys Thierry, 1690.

RÉGIS, PIERRE SYLVAIN, *L'Usage de la raison et de la foy, ou l'accord de la foy et de la raison.* Paris: Jean Cusson, 1704.

ROBINET, ANDRÉ. *Malebranche et Leibniz, relations personnelles, présentées avec les textes complets des auteurs et de leurs correspondants revus, corrigés et inédits.* Paris: J. Vrin, 1955.

ROCHOT, BERNARD. *Les Travaux de Gassendi sur Epicure et sur l'atomisme, 1619–1658.* Paris: J. Vrin, 1944.

ROHAULT, JACQUES. *Rohault's System of Natural Philosophy, Illustrated with Dr. Samuel Clarke's Notes taken mostly out of Sir Isaac Newton's Philosophy. With Additions.* Done into English by John Clarke. 2 volumes. London: James Knapton, 1723.

ROHAULT, JACQUES. *Traité de physique.* Paris: Vve de C. Savreux, 1671.

ROSENFIELD, LEONORA COHEN. *From Beast-Machine to Man-Machine.* New York: Oxford University Press. 1940.

SEBBA, GREGOR. *Bibliographia Cartesiana, A Critical Guide to the Descartes Literature 1800–1960,* International Archives of the History of Ideas 5, The Hague: M. Nijhoff, 1964.

SEBBA, GREGOR. *Nicolas Malebranche 1638–1715, A Preliminary Bibliography.* Athens, Georgia: The University of Georgia, 1959.

SEXTUS EMPIRICUS. *Sextus Empiricus with an English Translation.* Translated by R. G. Bury. 4 volumes. London: William Heinemann,. 1933–1939.

SMITH, NORMAN KEMP. *New Studies in the Philosophy of Descartes, Descartes as Pioneer.* London: Macmillan, 1952.

SMITH, NORMAN KEMP. *The Philosophy of David Hume, A Critical Study of its Origins and Central Doctrines.* London: Macmillan, 1941.
SMITH, NORMAN KEMP. *Studies in the Cartesian Philosophy.* London: Macmillan, 1902.
SORTAIS, GASTON. *La Philosophie moderne depuis Bacon jusqu'à Leibniz.* 2 volumes. Paris: Paul Lethielleux, 1920.
THOMAS, P.-FÉLIX. *La Philosophie de Gassendi.* Paris: Félix Alcan, 1889.
VERNON, THOMAS S. *The Metaphysical Role of Ideas in the Philosophy of Descartes.* Ann Arbor: University Microfilms, 1963.
YOLTON, JOHN W. *John Locke and the Way of Ideas.* Oxford: Oxford University Press, 1956.

ARTICLES

ALLAIRE, EDWIN B. "Existence, Independence, and Universals." *The Philosophical Review*, LXIX, 1960. 485–496.
ASCHENBRENNER, KARL. "Bishop Berkeley on Existence in the Mind" in *George Berkeley*, University of California Publications in Philosophy, XXIX. Berkeley and Los Angeles: University of California Press, 1957. 37–64.
BALZ, ALBERT G. A. "Clerselier, 1614–1684 and Rohault, 1620–1675," in *Cartesian Studies.* New York: Columbia University Press, 1951, 28–41.
BALZ, ALBERT G. A. "Louis de La Forge and the Critique of Substantial Forms," *Cartesian Studies.* New York: Columbia University Press, 1951, 80–104.
BERGMANN, GUSTAV. "Russell's Examination of Leibniz Examined," *Philosophy of Science*, XXIII, 1956, 175–203.
BERGMANN, GUSTAV. "Some Remarks on the Philosophy of Malebranche," *The Review of Metaphysics*, X, 1956, 207–225.
BOAS, MARIE. "Establishment of the Mechanical Philosophy," *Osiris*, X, 1952, 412–541
BRACKEN, HARRY M. "Berkeley and Malebranche on Ideas," *The Modern Schoolman*, XLI, 1963, 1–15.
BRACKEN, HARRY M. "Berkeley and Mental Acts," *Theoria*, XXVI, 1960, 140–146.
BRACKEN, HARRY M. "Berkeley's Realisms," *Philosophical Quarterly*, VIII, 1958, 1–15.
BUCHENAU, ARTHUR. "Idee und Perzeption. Ein Beitrag zur Ideenlehre Malebranches" in *Philosophische Abhandlungen, Herman Cohen zum 70. Geburtstag Dargebracht.* Berlin: Cassirer, 1912, 135–151.
BUCHENAU, ARTHUR. "Über Malebranches Lehre von der Wahrheit und ihre Bedeutung für die Methodik der Wissenschaften," *Archiv für die Geschichte der Philosophie*, XVI, 1910, 145–184.
CROMBIE, A. C. "Galileo Galilei: A Philosophical Symbol," in *Actes du VIIIe Congrès International d'Histoire des Sciences.* Florence: 3–9 September 1956, 1089–1095.
CUMMINS, PHILIP D. "Perceptual Relativity and Ideas in the Mind," *Philosophy and Phenomenological Research*, XXIV, 1963, 202–214.

FOUCHER, SIMON. "Extrait d'une lettre de M. Foucher chanoine de Dijon, pour repondre à M. de Leibniz sur quelques axiomes de philosophie," *Journal des sçavans* (Amsterdam), XXI (16 mars 1693), 182–186.

FOUCHER, SIMON. "Réponse de M. S. F. à M. de L. B. Z. sur son nouveau sisteme de la communication des substances, proposé dans les journaux du 27 juin & du 4 juillet 1695," *Journal des sçavans* (Amsterdam), XXIII (12 septembre 1695), 639–645.

FRITZ, ANITA D. "Berkeley's Self–Its Origin in Malebranche," *Journal of the History of Ideas*, XV, 1954, 554–572.

FRITZ, ANITA D. "Malebranche and Immaterialism of Berkeley," *The Review of Metaphysics*, III, 1949–1950, 59–80.

GOUHIER, HENRI. "La Première polémique de Malebranche," *Revue d'histoire de la philosophie*, I, 1927, 23–48, 168–191.

KOYRÉ, ALEXANDRE. "Galileo and Plato," *Journal of the History of Ideas*, IV, 1943, 400–428.

KOYRÉ, ALEXANDRE. "Galileo and the Scientific Revolution of the XVII Century," *The Philosophical Review*, LII, 1943, 333–348.

LAPORTE, JEAN. "La Connaissance de l'étendue chez Descartes," in *Études d'histoire de la philosophie française au XVIIe siècle*. Paris: J. Vrin, 1951, 11–36.

LAPORTE, JEAN. "L'Étendue intelligible selon Malebranche," in *Études d'histoire de la philosophie française au XVIIe siècle*. Paris: J. Vrin, 1951, 153–193.

LEIBNIZ, GOTTFRIED WILHELM. "Eclaircissement du nouveau systeme de la communication des substances, pour servir de reponse à ce qui en a été dit dans le journal du 12 sept. 1695," *Journal des sçavans* (Amsterdam), XXIV (2 et 9 avril 1696), 255–258, 259–263.

LEIBNIZ, GOTTFRIED WILHELM. "Excerpta ex notis meis inauguralibus ad Fucherii responsionem in Malebranchium critica" in Rabbe, *Étude philosophique*, XL–XLII; "Notes on the Reply of Foucher to the Criticism of his Criticism of the *Recherche de la verité*," in *Philosophical Papers and Letters*, ed. Loemker, 241–242.

LEIBNIZ, GOTTFRIED WILHELM. "Extrait d'une lettre de Monsr. de Leibniz à Mr. Foucher chanoine de Dijon, sur quelques axiomes de philosophie," *Journal des sçavans* (Amsterdam), XX (2 juin 1692), 365–369.

LEIBNIZ, GOTTFRIED WILHELM. "De Ipsi Nature sive de Vi Insita, Actionibusque Creaturarum; pro Dynamicus suis confirmandis illustrandisque," *Acta eruditorum Lipsiensum* (septembre 1698), 427–440; "On Nature Itself, or on the Inherent Force and Actions of Created Things to Serve to Confirm and Illustrate the Author's Dynamics." *Acta eruditorum Lipsiensum*, septembre 1698, in *Philosophical Papers and Letters*, ed. Loemker, 808–824.

LEIBNIZ, GOTTFRIED WILHELM. "Meditationes de Cognitione, Veritate et Ideis," *Acta eruditorum Lipsiensum*, (novembre, 1684), 537–542; in *Schriften*, IV, Gerhardt, 422–426; "Meditations on Knowledge, Truth, and Ideas," *Acta eruditorum Lipsiensum*, novembre 1684, in *Philosophical Papers and Letters*, ed. Loemker, 448–481.

LEIBNIZ, GOTTFRIED WILHELM. "De Modo Distinguendi Phaenomena Realia ab Imaginariis," in *Schriften*, ed. Gerhardt: VII, 319–322; "On the

Method of Distinguishing Real from Imaginary Phenomena," Date unknown, in *Philosophical Papers and Letters*, ed. Loemker, 602–607.

LEIBNIZ, GOTTFRIED WILHELM. "Primae Veritates" in *Opuscles et fragments*, ed. Couteret, 518–523; "First Truths", Ca. 1680–1684, in *Philosophical Papers and Letters*, ed. Loemker, 411–417.

LEIBNIZ, GOTTFRIED WILHELM. "Quid sit Idea" in Gerhardt: *Schriften*, VII, 263–264; "What is an Idea?," 1678, in *Philosophical Papers and Letters*, ed. Loemker, 317–329.

LEIBNIZ, GOTTFRIED WILHELM. "Réponse de Mr. de Leibniz à l'extrait de la lettre de Mr. Foucher chanoine de Dijon, insérée dans le journal du 16 mars 1693," *Journal des sçavans* (Amsterdam), XXI (3 aoust 1693), 527–529.

LEIBNIZ, GOTTFRIED WILHELM. "Sistême nouveau de la nature & de la communication des substances, aussi bien que de l'union qu'il y a entre l'ame & le corps. Par M. D. L.", *Journal des sçavans* (Amsterdam), XXIII (27 juin & 4 juillet 1695), 444–454, 455–462.

LENOBLE, ROBERT. "Origines de la pensée scientifique moderne," in *Encyclopédie de la Pléiade, Histoire de la science*. Tome V. Paris: Gallimard, 1957, 369–534.

LOUGH, JOHN. "Locke's Reading during his Stay in France," *The Library, A Quarterly Review of Bibliography, Transactions of the Bibliographical Society*, Third Series, VIII, 1953, 229–258.

LOVEJOY, A. O. "'Representative Ideas' in Malebranche and Arnauld," *Mind*, XXXII, 1923, 449–464.

POPKIN, RICHARD H. "L'Abbé Foucher et le problème des qualités premières," *Bulletin de la Société d'Étude du XVIIe Siècle*, N° 33, 1957, 633–647.

POPKIN, RICHARD H. "Berkeley and Pyrrhonism," *Review of Metaphysics*, V, 1951, 1952, 223–246.

POPKIN, RICHARD H. "David Hume and the Pyrrhonian Controversy," *Review of Metaphysics*, VI, 1952–1953, 65–81.

POPKIN, RICHARD H. "David Hume: His Pyrrhonism and his Critique of Pyrrhonism," *Philosophical Quarterly*, I, 1950–1951, 385–407.

POPKIN, RICHARD H. "Did Hume ever Read Berkeley?", *The Journal of Philosophy*, LVI, 1959, 535–545.

POPKIN, RICHARD H. "The High Road to Pyrrhonism", *American Philosophical Quarterly*, II, 1965, 18–32.

POPKIN, RICHARD H. "The New Realism of Bishop Berkeley," in *George Berkeley*, University of California Publications in Philosophy, XXIX. Berkeley and Los Angeles: University of California Press, 1957, 1–19.

POPKIN, RICHARD H. "The Sceptical Crisis and the Rise of Modern Philosophy, III," *Review of Metaphysics*, VII, 1953–1954, 499–510.

POPKIN, RICHARD H. "The Sceptical Precursors of David Hume," *Philosophy and Phenomenological Research*, XVI, 1955, 61–71.

POPKIN, RICHARD H. "So, Hume Did Read Berkeley," *Journal of Philosophy*, LXI, 1964, 773–778.

ROSENFIELD, LEONORA COHEN. "Peripatetic Adversaries of Cartesianism in 17th Century France," *Review of Religion*, XXII, 1957, 14–40.

TURNBULL, ROBERT G. "Aseity and Dependence in Leibniz's Metaphysics," *Theoria*, XXV, 1959, 95–114.

WATSON, RICHARD A. "Berkeley in a Cartesian Context," *Revue internationale de philosophie*, N° 65, 1963, 381–394.

WATSON, RICHARD A. "The Breakdown of Cartesian Metaphysics," *Journal of the History of Philosophy*, I, 1964, 177–197.

WATSON, RICHARD A. "A Note on the Probabilistic Physics of Régis," *Archives internationales d'histoire des sciences*, N° 66, 1964, pp. 33–36.

YOLTON, JOHN W. "Locke and the Seventeenth-Century Logic of Ideas," *Journal of the History of Ideas*, XVI, 1955, 431–452.

# INDEX OF NAMES